CONFIRMATION TRAINING

CONFIRMATION TRAINING

A Handbook for those preparing
Candidates for Confirmation

By

DENIS E. TAYLOR, M.A.

Lately Dean of Brisbane; former Director of General
Board of Religious Education of the Church of England
in Australia, Youth and Education Secretary of the
British Council of Churches

Author of
*In His Presence, God's Family, Here We Offer,
Serving at the Altar, etc.*

THE RELIGIOUS EDUCATION PRESS, LTD.
(A member of the Pergamon Group)
HEADINGTON HILL HALL   OXFORD

First Published 1961
Second Edition 1967

PRINTED IN GREAT BRITAIN BY COX AND WYMAN, LTD.
LONDON, FAKENHAM AND READING
6059/61

CONTENTS

ACKNOWLEDGMENTS

This book was planned some years ago. In 1956, while still in Australia, I suggested it to Mr. Ernest H. Hayes to whose sympathy, enterprise and skill as a publisher my earlier books on Confirmation and the Holy Communion—*In His Presence, God's Family* and *Here We Offer*—owe much.

Every writer, however, knows how wide is the gap between the planning stage and final achievement. It was the encouragement of Canon F. S. Popham, M.A., M.Ed., Ph.D., Chairman of Children's Committee of York Provincial Council of Religious Education, which provided the extra spur needed to produce this book. I wish to acknowledge here with gratitude the care and thought which he has most freely expended in reading and criticising not only *Confirmation Training* but also the three earlier books mentioned above.

I have not accepted all his suggestions and we have not always seen eye to eye, but I am conscious of many pitfalls avoided through his wisdom, and am grateful for many helpful suggestions which have sprung from his wide experience and scholarship. From these my books have benefited and, one hopes, with them the whole cause of religious education.

To Canon Popham's lifelong enthusiasm for this cause, and the great services he has rendered, it is a privilege and pleasure to be allowed to pay tribute.

DENIS E. TAYLOR.

NOTE

These instructions are a complete course of Confirmation Training in themselves.

They have, however, been specially designed for use where either

IN HIS PRESENCE

or

GOD'S FAMILY

are presented to the candidate at the beginning of the Confirmation Course. These books are referred to and are used throughout, both as a summary of the instructions and as a basis for devotional training.

P.S. Page references to *In His Presence* in the text of this book relate to the present revised edition. Readers who possess earlier editions of that book can trace these references through the *List of Contents*.

FOREWORD

by

THE VERY REVEREND THE DEAN OF LLANDAFF

CONFIRMATION INSTRUCTION is one of the greatest and most valuable opportunities that come the way of a Parish Priest. I believe that the clergy to-day are anxious, as never before, to make the most of it; yet at the end of each course I imagine that most of us feel dissatisfied. There is always the difficulty of striking a happy balance between the teaching that we feel must now or never be driven home and, on the other hand, the inculcating of habits of prayer, worship, Communion, and self-discipline that may grow and develop.

For many years I have found *In His Presence* an admirable Confirmation Manual, because it has kept this balance so well, and I have based my syllabus largely on its contents. I am therefore more than delighted to know that its author has now drawn up a syllabus of Confirmation Classes based entirely on this Manual which can be used as a book of reference throughout the classes.

I feel certain that a great many post-Confirmation lapses can be avoided if we resist the temptation to think that the whole of the Christian Faith has to be taught in three months at the expense of the practical application of it in obedience to a Rule of Life. I believe whole-heartedly in the truth of our Lord's words:

'If any man will do His will, he shall know of the doctrine' (St. John 7. 17).

It is in doing it that we gradually experience the truth of the Christian Faith.

Though each one will wish to add or subtract in the use of this book, I am convinced that it will be of inestimable value, both in the preparation of children and adults, and will help to set their feet more firmly on the paths of loyalty and discipline in the service of God and His Church.

E. S. THOMAS.

INTRODUCTION

A New Strategy

Preparation for Confirmation is vital. In these days when Bible Classes are rare, the brief Confirmation course is the last systematised instruction which very many young Anglicans receive. Lucky are the few, but they are very few, who receive a serious course of teaching in Youth Group or Fellowship. Sermons are too often more of a hortatory rather than of a teaching character and seldom follow a consistent course. And in any case Confirmation, instead of being the beginning of an active communicant Church membership, so often is the climax of Church life, after which all too soon the newly confirmed youngster follows the example of Dad and Mum and becomes a Harvest Thanksgiving, Easter and Christmas Christian; probably in that order.

How vital then those precious months of preparation for Confirmation!

Yet, how dreadfully unsatisfactory, from an educational standpoint, is the practice in the average Anglican parish. Anyone who has done any teaching at all knows that, when the revision lesson comes along, the humiliating discovery is made that at least 50 per cent of what has been so carefully and patiently taught has been forgotten already, and much of what has been retained is remembered only in a jumbled and inaccurate form. And that is within a few weeks of the lesson! How much then will be remembered after one year or five?

The purpose of this book is to set out a very simple change of strategy which any parish priest can adopt without any difficulty whatsoever. It is based on the age-old principle that what is seen with the eye is remembered much more fully than that which is heard only. Whilst setting out a thorough course of instruction, it is believed that the inculcation of good habits is as important or even more important than a mere knowledge of facts.

The custom in many parishes is for the Confirmation candidate to be given a little Manual of Devotion when the Confirmation takes place. It is meant, of course, to be used from then onwards. In practice it gets put away carefully as a souvenir or memento of the occasion, and rarely taken out of the bottom drawer again.

How simple, and how much more effective:

1. To give a suitable manual which combines devotion and instruction at the *first* meeting of the Confirmation Class;

2. To train the candidate in the use of the devotional parts of that manual throughout the course, thus trying to begin the formation of habits of prayer, and Bible reading, and the keeping of a very simple rule of life;

3. To use the instructional sections of the manual as a text book, to which reference is made in the classes constantly. Each section then forms both a summary and a book of reference for every subject taught.

In His Presence was written nineteen years ago for this purpose, and this plan has stood the test of time. Used in this way it is suitable for teenager or adult.

God's Family is a junior version of the same book, designed to interest and attract the younger Confirmation candidates, the tens to twelves. Although, obviously, it is desirable to teach a child of 11 and an adolescent of 15 separately, the writer has found it easy and reasonably satisfactory when necessary to have a group of about twenty young people, the juniors using *God's Family* and the older ones, slightly flattered by being given the senior book, *In His Presence*. A happy and keen class has ensued.

The outline of procedure and instruction in the chapters which follow is aimed at forming habits of daily prayer and Bible reading; of preparation for Holy Communion; of instructed and understanding worship in the Liturgy, and of thanksgiving afterwards. In capable hands, it will lay a foundation of knowledge and chart out a track for daily living, likely to produce well-taught and devout communicants who understand and love their Lord and His Church.

Hints on Teaching

At the University a professor *lectures* and students may take down notes, but rarely speak or ask questions.

In school a teacher *teaches* by short instructions (never long lectures), by visual aids (blackboard, pictures, text books, etc.) and by questioning. He keeps his class constantly alert by giving them things to look up, by asking them questions, by writing brief notes or doing drawings.

Real concentration for more than a minute or two is difficult for children—and for many adults, too. Short sentences, a snappy, vigorous and sometimes witty method of 'attack' or 'putting it over', frequent questioning, fostering competition in answering, looking up references—all these help to keep the class alive and alert. Avoid lecturing like the plague. Some youngsters may appear to be paying attention—but after a few minutes their thoughts are probably far away even if their eyes are still on the speaker.

Evolve from the lesson a brief formula or summary whenever possible, which may be repeated frequently.

Constant revision is essential for the pupil and most chastening to the pride of the teacher.

Many teachers will want candidates to have a notebook and will dictate very brief summaries. These have not been given in this book because so many classes meet where writing is difficult, e.g., in chairs or pews in church, and because both *God's Family* and *In His Presence* are in effect their own summaries. But where writing is possible and does not take too much time, very short dictated notes help to 'fix' a lesson. But this is very time-consuming.

The style adopted throughout this book is a deliberate

attempt to reflect the quick and constant changes from statement to question, etc., which a good teacher uses all the time, keeping the class alert and interested. Smooth flowing periods and well-constructed sentences will lull a class to drowsiness in no time. It is hoped that there are few in this book. It is meant to help the teacher to teach, not the parson to lecture, and its text is meant to reflect the mercurial changes the teacher will deliberately practise.

Filmstrips for Supplementary Use and with the Congregation*

Filmstrips, if judiciously chosen and used with skill (and this is not too easy) can be an effective adjunct in confirmation training. It is only as an adjunct—though a valuable one—that their use is advocated in this training course, and not as a substitute for any part of it. Many people can remember what they have seen more readily and completely than that which they have heard only. As well as assisting the memory, filmstrips can also help those who are slow in forming the mental images which the spoken word is intended to convey.

The way to use filmstrips in confirmation training is the important question. The writer has tried using strips at the actual classes to supplement the instructions given to the candidates. He has also experimented

* All or any of these can be obtained from Carwal, Ltd. the Visual Aid branch of The Religious Education Press, Limited.

in using them with the congregation and the candidates in church in a definite endeavour to interest the congregation in what the candidates were studying, and, without saying so, to remedy some of the appalling gaps in the knowledge of the average member of the congregation.

This latter method has undoubtedly much to recommend it. It is explained at the start of the classes that Evensong with these filmstrips is part of the course of training, and that the attendance of candidates is required. The general congregation thoroughly appreciate the strips and feel that they have a real responsibility and share in the course, and can be led to pray with much more interest and zeal both in church and privately for the candidates. Usually, a number of the parents of candidates can be induced quite readily to attend both to encourage the children and also as a refresher course for themselves.

The strips suggested below are by no means the only ones available or suitable. They are listed as being really first-rate and also as fitting well at those particular points in the course. They are available either for hire or purchase and priests are recommended to study the list of strips, compiled from many sources, which is published by the S.P.C.K. entitled *A.V.A. Guide*, price 1s. 6d. Another most valuable quarterly is *A.V.A.*, published by R.E.P. Film Bureau, (price 1s 6d). Any of the strips mentioned below can be purchased from R.E.P. supply dept. Carwal Ltd. All prices subject to alteration without notice.

Fitting Filmstrips into the Training

Any priest who wants to use filmstrips should make himself familiar with Canon A. J. Watts' series *The Revised Catechism*. There are seven strips in the series: *Membership, Belief, God to the Rescue, Obedience, Grace, Sacraments* and *The Bible and Christian Hope*. Most have about 30 frames, are in colour and cost 21s. each or £6 6s. od. for the set.

After a weekday meeting of the class the appropriate strip from this series could be used at Evensong on Sunday with equal value and interest to the congregation and the candidates. In the framework of the Catechism some of the essential elements of the Christian Faith are taught visually as well as verbally: belonging, believing, duty to God, duty to man, God's gift of grace through prayer and sacraments, the offering of the whole life to God. We all know how much more deep an impression is made by that which is absorbed through the eye-gate than that which is taught by word of mouth only.

Preparation of new candidates becomes, through the use of filmstrips on Sunday evenings, a valuable refresher course for those confirmed maybe many years ago, and this without them realising it. In effect, if skilfully handled, it can become almost a teaching mission to the congregation as well as a very real help to the candidates.

Here is a suggested order for fitting filmstrips into the Confirmation Training:

B

1. Immediately before the start of classes show the strip *Into the Church* Part 2. *Confirmation and First Communion.* (S.P.C.K. No. 1211, 34 frames. 12s. 6d. Notes by the Rev. F. Noel Davey.)

When the candidates have been collected, on the Sunday before the classes start, use this strip in church with candidates and congregation, parents of the candidates having been specially invited. In the filmstrip a lad joins the Confirmation class and receives instruction in the Catechism. The Confirmation service is followed in detail and, after his first Communion, the boy learns the duties of Church membership.

2. On the next two or three Sunday evenings the earlier strips of the series *The Revised Catechism* fit in admirably. They supplement the teaching given in the classes without going over the same ground unduly, or do so in a quite different way. They will make an impression because of the striking illustrations.

3. To supplement the instruction at the fourth meeting of the class the strip on Baptism, *Dost Thou . . .?* (No. 1215. 35 frames. Colour. 21s.) may be used in church with candidates and congregation. Originally produced in a parish in the north of England this strip sets out to demonstrate—largely by coloured cartoons —the importance of Infant Baptism. The physical and spiritual sides of our natures are contrasted and the need for spiritual training and spiritual food is shown just as clearly as the need for physical and mental training for the material things of life.

4. Several meetings of the Confirmation class are devoted to the Holy Communion. (Meetings 9–12). Members are beginning to look forward to their first Communion. Now is the time to show some of the excellent strips available on the Liturgy. *Draw Near* (S.P.C.K. No. 1213. 48 frames. Colour. 22s. 6d. Teaching Notes by Canon Watts.) In this strip vestments are used. The parallel strip, *Our Bounden Duty* (S.P.C.K. No. 1214. 42 frames. Colour. 22s. 6d. Teaching Notes by A. W. Dowle.) uses surplice and stole.

Whichever of this pair is used, it could be preceded the week before with selections from the *Revised Catechism* series by Canon Watts to supply more background. *Draw Near* and *Our Bounden Duty* have excellent notes and these dovetail in extremely well with the instruction in this book. Every stage of the action of the Liturgy is shown in detail and the notes stress the 'shape' of the Eucharist, what its action expresses as well as its words. The teaching on the Offertory in the notes on *Draw Near* fits particularly well with the aspects stressed in this book.

5. *It Could Make the Difference*. No. 1, *At Holy Communion*. (S.P.C.K. No. 1203. 45 frames. 15s. Notes by the Rev. F. Noel Davey.) This strip fits in well at the conclusion of the classes after Preparation for Holy Communion has been carefully taught. Or it might be used either for the first time, or shown again, shortly after First Communion. It stresses with a light touch

the difference careful preparation makes, shows the importance of such elementary good habits as punctuality, and has practical hints on how to concentrate, how to pray, the correct attitude in kneeling, receiving the consecrated elements, etc. The touch of humour makes its seriousness all the more effective. Once again, most valuable for *both* general congregation and candidates.

Sponsors at Confirmation

This use of filmstrips in training for Confirmation seems calculated to create a bond of mutual interest and understanding between candidates and congregation; a link strengthened by thought, study and prayer, shared together over several months. If wisely handled this might well lead on to the atmosphere necessary to make a success of the system of candidates each having a 'sponsor' at Confirmation, whose duty it is to encourage and help them to persevere in the first crucial months and years of their life as communicants. This is outlined in the rubrics of the Scottish Prayer Book 1929, and at least a hint of it is given in '1662.' 'And every one shall have a Godfather or a Godmother as a Witness of their Confirmation.' (Rubric after Catechism.) See 14th Meeting of class.

First Meeting of Class

THE MEANING OF CONFIRMATION

You will need:

1. *Roll-book* prepared for:
   a. Names and addresses,
   b. Ages,
   c. Date of Baptism.
   d. Attendance Register.

2. Copies of *In His Presence* or *God's Family* for each candidate.

Emphasise that these books *must* be brought to every meeting. Suggest that a paper cover be added to keep them fresh and clean, because they are going to become very important.

3. *Prayer Book and Bible.*

Opening Prayer. Sometimes one or two collects may be said, sometimes a brief extempore prayer. It is important to have variety to maintain freshness. It may be found that prayer comes more easily and naturally at the close of the instruction than at the start. Other priests may wish to have both. Much depends on whether the group is meeting in the church or in a hall or room.

    a. Get names, addresses, ages.

    b. Ask whether baptised or not. Some may not know. Ask them to find out at home and report at next meeting.

    c. Mark attendance register.

    d. Issue manuals. Tell members to write their names in these when they get home.

Aim of Instruction:

To teach what Confirmation is, and why people should be confirmed.

What is Confirmation?

It is God's gift to us of the Holy Spirit to strengthen us for our life's work, and enable us to live as Christ's men and women. It is the fulfilment of the promise Jesus made: 'I will not leave you strengthless (comfortless), I will come to you'—'fort' in com*fort*less, —'firm' in con*firm*ation—come from the Latin word for strength. Jesus comes to us in Spirit to-day to dwell in us, just as nineteen and a half centuries ago He came in the flesh to live among and work with and strengthen people in Nazareth and Bethlehem and Jerusalem. He comes to strengthen us and make us increasingly His own.

We desperately need strengthening. The older we get the more difficult life becomes; problems are harder, temptations stronger. Our Heavenly Father knows that. But it is God's way that just as anything worth while has to be worked for, e.g., skill at sport demands training and practice, skill at music demands ever so many hours of scales and practice, so spiritual strength, strength of character, the ability to be a person of use to God, is not given to us by God unless we want it and work for it. It is God who makes us want it. It is God who helps us to work for it and encourages us all the way; but we must work for it. Confirmation preparation is a time of special effort.

Repeat: Confirmation is God's wonderful gift of the Holy Spirit, the Spirit of Jesus, who said 'I will not leave you strengthless. I will come to you.'

Now some questions:

Must I be confirmed? No—of course not. Run away home if you do not *want* God's wonderful gift. There is *no* compulsion. But: you *must* be confirmed if you wish to be a communicant, that is one who is privileged to receive the Sacrament of the Holy Communion. Holy Communion is far too serious, too sacred to allow just anybody to come. Communicants must be trying to be better people. They must prepare and make themselves ready carefully. They must *know* more.

When you were baptised your godparents promised solemnly to God in Church that they would see that you were 'brought to the Bishop to be confirmed by him so that *strengthened with the gift of the Holy Spirit*' you might 'come with due preparation to receive the blessed Sacrament of the Body and Blood of Christ, and go forth into the world to serve God faithfully in the fellowship of His Church.' (See Duties of Godparents stated near end of *Public Baptism of Infants.*) Let class look this up. If they have not brought Prayer Books emphasise that Prayer Book and *In His Presence* or *God's Family* must be brought next time.

Now teach four 'quickies' to end this section: Why be Confirmed?

1. Because it is in the Bible.

The reference from Chapter 8 of the Acts of the Apostles is set out in *In His Presence*, p. 28; *God's Family*, p. 10. Turn to those pages and we will read it.

If your Aunt Jemima, or other very superior person, sniffs and says 'I am sure I don't know why you want to be confirmed—*I* never was; we don't have it in *my* Church.' (Whether such a remark is made by a Methodist, Baptist, Congregationalist, Presbyterian or Plymouth Brother maybe), you have the perfect answer: 'I am going to be confirmed *because it is in the Bible.*' That is the first reason: because it is in the Bible.

2. Because it has been in the Church from the beginning . . . see *God's Family*, p. 10.

3. Because we need to be made FIRMer. God strengthens us by the Holy Spirit.

4. Because ConFIRMation is the doorway to Holy Communion.

Rehearse these four 'quickies' and discuss them until the group is word-perfect. Be sure they know the reference in Acts of the Apostles (ch. 8). Say you will ask them again next week, so they must learn them at home from *In His Presence* or *God's Family*.

What Happens at Confirmation? *You* do something; *God* does something.

You take on your own shoulders the promises made for you by your godparents at baptism.

God gives you the strength to keep these tremendous promises by sending you the Holy Spirit.

Now—we'll learn these three promises, three mighty promises.

You promise to try your very best with God's help:

1. To give up what is wrong;

2. To believe what is true (about God and His world). This is summed up in '*the Articles of the Christian Faith*,' especially the Creed;

3. To do what is right—obey God's Holy will and Commandments.

Rehearse these three promises until the group has thoroughly memorised them.

See if they can repeat the Apostles' Creed (for '*the Articles of the Christian Faith*'). Do they know the Ten Commandments? Insist that for next class they be word-perfect in the Apostles' Creed. Repeat references in *God's Family* and *In His Presence*.

Note: Remind those who could not give them to bring particulars next week of the place and date of their Baptism.

Attendance at Worship

At an early meeting of the class, probably the first, or certainly no later than the second, the question of the candidates' rule of attendance at church services must be considered. Parish priests will make different arrangements according to the pattern of worship in that parish.

It is enough here to point out four things:

1. Regular attendance at not less than one service every Sunday must be regarded as essential.

2. When there is a Parish Communion this will probably be chosen.

3. In all types of parish it should be arranged that candidates attend Communion or Eucharist before teaching about the Liturgy is reached in their preparation class (without of course receiving the Sacrament). It is extremely difficult to teach how to worship at this supreme Service until those being taught are familiar with its content and procedure.

4. It is suggested that the ideal to be taught each member of the class is attendance at the Parish Communion week by week, and a return to Evensong to give thanks.

As has been so often pointed out, those who attend Holy Communion only will hear only a very limited selection of Holy Scripture read and taught.

Second Meeting of Class

LEARNING TO PRAY

You will need:

Roll Book, Confirmation Manuals, Prayer Book and Bible.

Note: Complete the record of the Baptism particulars of each candidate.

Aim: *a. To create or reinforce the habit of daily prayer;*

b. To teach the four parts of prayer: Adoration, Confession, Thanksgiving, Supplication;

c. To start members using regularly the prayer sections of God's Family *and* In His Presence.

Why be confirmed?

After opening prayer, start with a brief revision: What is Confirmation? The gift by God to us of His Holy Spirit.

Why be confirmed?—The 'four quickies':

a. Is in the Bible (Acts Ch. 8),

b. Has been in the Church from the beginning,

c. Makes us FIRMer,

d. Is the gateway to Holy Communion.

What happens in Confirmation?—God does something. We do something—

27

   a. God gives the Holy Spirit,
   b. We take upon our own shoulders the very
      serious promises made on our behalf by our
      godparents at Baptism.

What are the Three Promises?

   a. To renounce,
   b. To believe,
   c. To obey.

Who can repeat the Apostles' Creed? Say that later
on we shall examine each statement in the Creed.

Ten minutes on this 'drill' is time well spent, and
the class will enjoy it.

Explain that your job as parish priest is to give the
class facts and information, and these are essential.

But the real preparation for Confirmation is something which each candidate can only do for himself or
herself. No amount of knowledge of facts makes a
person ready to be confirmed; only the effort made by
each to become a better person by striving to know and
love God more through prayer and Bible study and
worship, and by fighting to overcome besetting sins and
temptations. It is what we do for ourselves that really
counts in preparing for Confirmation. Unless we are
determined to make a real effort in this direction it is
dishonest to go on to Confirmation.

Prayer is a Relationship

In this class we are going to think about our prayers.
'Religion' means a tie or bond or relationship. A
relationship, that is, between each of us and Jesus.

Is there any such relationship in your life? For some people to-day 'Jesus Christ' is just a swear word. For others, He is a shadowy figure of the dim and distant past. For others, God's Son, Very God of Very God. For others, an Unseen, but none the less real, friend. A person we can know and love and talk to, someone who matters supremely.

Your own preparation for Confirmation consists in laying the beginnings of that personal friendship and relationship with our Lord. That is 'religion,' your relationship with Jesus.

There cannot be any real friendship or relationship between people unless there is communication between them.

My best friends are on the other side of the world, but we remain friends because we are in regular communication (by letter).

Our links with Jesus are Worship (when we give Him some of our time and love), the Bible where we read about Him and give Him a chance to speak to us in our minds, and chiefly and above all, Prayer.

Great numbers of grown-up people have never learned to pray. If they pray at all, their prayers are older versions of what they learned at their mother's knee. 'God bless daddy and mummy and make me a good boy, for Jesus Christ's sake. Amen.' Quite a good prayer for a very little child—but very little use for an adult. No wonder such people give up praying and fall away from God's family the Church.

In our books we are going to *learn* now the four chief

parts of prayer and then we are going to practise making prayers to that pattern—see *God's Family*, p. 4; *In His Presence*, p. 8.

We'll learn these four parts of prayers first. Note that their first letters form the word ACTS. That helps us always to remember them.

ADORATION expresses our *love* and *wonder* and *reverence* and *awe* and *humility* and *praise* before the majesty and beauty and loveliness and goodness and love of God, made known to us in Jesus. Some people tend to think about God as a dear old gentleman in carpet slippers, far too kind ever to punish. The people in the Bible were much wiser. They had a healthy fear and awe of God. They knew He puts up with no nonsense—no wickedness. They knew He is a terrible but all-just judge.

God is the great power that has brought into existence this incredibly wonderful Universe and this earth with all its amazing forces which to-day science is discovering one by one. Just the latest are nuclear fission, the invisible etheric waves used for radio and TV, the near-miracles of space research. God created all these forces, and greater wonders still to be discovered, when He made the earth. And not only the earth, but sun and moon and stars and space and light. Our minds cannot grasp its wonders. Light travels at 186,000 miles a second. Yet space is so vast that it takes hundreds of years for light travelling at that incredible speed to reach this earth from some of the stars. This

Creator God, who is also our Father God, and made us to have a very special and unique place in His universe, this is the God of incredible wonder whom we worship.

(Along some such lines try to arouse a sense of wonder and humility before the mystery of God.)

Is it surprising that our prayers start with ADORA-TION? So we begin to pray by telling God something of our wonder and love. *In His Presence*, pp. 14 and 15, has some splendid words of adoration. Let's look at them. (Members may read them in turn.)

Can we think of others? They must be addressed *to* God. If members' Prayer Books include a Hymnal, many examples may be found there. The Psalms are a rich source of acts of adoration.

CONFESSION is the second part of prayer.

A sense of all that God is and all that He does for us at once brings home to us our unworthiness, how often we fail to live up even to our own poor ideals, how feeble our fight against temptation, how weak our efforts to do the good things we could and should have done but alas did not.

What are some of the commonest sins? Draw out a list from members. Suggest they turn to *God's Family*, pp. 29, 30; *In His Presence*, pp. 65–67. Point out that there are sins of omission as well as wrongful thoughts and words and deeds. So we tell God our sins and ask His forgiveness. *God's Family*, p. 4, suggests the way we can do this, and the kind of words to use. Or in *In His Presence*, p. 11. Let's look at these carefully.

Forgiveness can be ours only because of God's love

and because of what Jesus has done for us, and so the next part of prayer is naturally

THANKSGIVING—a 'joyful and pleasant thing it is to be thankful.' A person who counts his blessings and thanks God for them is always a happy, cheerful person with the right kind of outlook on life.

Unthankful people nine times out of ten become grizzlers and grousers, discontented, unhappy, never satisfied, a misery to themselves and a pain in the neck to others. Thanksgiving is a fundamental part of Christian character.

So, on our knees each night, we spend a few minutes counting up our blessings and saying 'Thank You' to God. *God's Family*, p. 5; *In His Presence*, p. 12.

The fourth part of prayer, the part that everybody knows, is asking. The technical name is

SUPPLICATION, asking God for things. Technically, *intercession* when we ask on behalf of others; *petition* when we ask for ourselves. Let's look again at *God's Family*, p. 6; *In His Presence*, p. 13.

Now, let's practise these four parts, A-C-T-S, and think of examples of each.

All this may take a lot of time to talk about or learn, but to do this is perfectly easy and just becomes second nature.

Can you remember the four parts? A: Adoration. C: Confession. T: Thanksgiving. S: Supplication, or simply, just asking your Heavenly Father, for others and for ourselves.

The absolute bed-rock of our Confirmation preparation is the use of this system. We can study it in *In His Presence* (or *God's Family*) and we must go on doing it all our life, so that we can no more think of going to bed at night without praying like this than we could go to bed without taking our clothes off. BUT—a good hint—pray *before* you take your clothes off. There is no virtue in getting cold.

Note: For next week copies of the Bible Reading Fellowship booklet of Readings for Confirmation Candidates 'House on the Rock' will be required. Order from: The Bible Reading Fellowship, 148, Buckingham Palace Road, London, S.W.1. The cost; 6d. per copy.

Third Meeting of Class

THE PLACE OF THE BIBLE

You will need:

Roll Book, Confirmation Manuals, Prayer Book and Bible, Bible Reading Fellowship booklets 'House on the Rock', F.W.O. or similar envelopes.

Aim: *To strengthen the habit of daily prayer; to begin forming the habit of daily Bible reading, and to explain a simple rule of life.*

(*Note:* Opening and/or closing prayers are not mentioned from now on. It is assumed that these are taking place.)

Revision

Let's get alive and alert by some high-speed drill. First about last week:

What are the four parts of Prayer? (Adoration, Confession, Thanksgiving, Supplication.)

What does 'religion' mean? (Tie, bond or relationship.) One example of words of adoration?

What was the promise of Jesus: 'I will not leave you . . .? (comfortless). I will come to you.' What does that word mean? (strengthless).

What is Confirmation? (Gift of the Holy Spirit to us by God.)

What do *we* do at Confirmation? (We re-affirm the promise to a. Renounce; b. Believe; c. Obey.)

What does *God* do? (He gives us His Holy Spirit.)

What must we believe? (Articles of the Christian faith contained in the *Creed*.)

Why should we be confirmed? Four 'quickies'?

   a. Because Confirmation is in the Bible,
   b. Because it has been in the Church from the beginning,
   c. Because it makes us *firmer*,
   d. Because it is the gateway to the Holy Communion.

Ten minutes of such drill is well spent.

Prayer

Now I want to ask you how you have been getting on with modelling your prayers on the A-C-T-S pattern? (This is of bed-rock importance. Satisfy yourself that each member is making a real effort in this. Little can be achieved unless and until members really are trying to pray better.)

If it is in accord with their age and ability, ask each to bring you next week under A-C-T-S headings a very brief specimen of what a person's evening prayers *might* be, not necessarily their own.

Talk to them about *where* they pray. Does it help to be kneeling in imagination at the foot of the Cross?

Some boys and girls have bought a cross or crucifix

for the wall of their bedroom and make a little shrine or prayer corner where they kneel, adding one or two good pictures.

Discuss the difficulty of wandering thoughts and how to bring one's mind back to Jesus by turning each wandering thought into a prayer. E.g., when you are trying to concentrate you suddenly find you have started to think instead about John Smith next door. Say a prayer for him to Jesus and so bring your mind back to our Lord. Kneeling upright instead of leaning over the side of the bed, and holding our hands in the attitude of prayer can often help surprisingly in the effort to concentrate and to be more aware of God's presence.

Reading the Bible

Explain that if, during these months of preparation for Confirmation, candidates can form—and of course, keep—the twin habits of daily prayer and daily reading of the Bible, God's holy word, then this period is one of the most profitable in their whole life. We to-day are rather unlucky. If we had lived fifty years ago—or very probably if we were to live fifty years on—we should have found that most people read the Bible if not every day at least far more often than most do to-day. Fifty years ago very many families had family prayers in the home conducted every day by the head of the family. But social patterns of behaviour change. Daily reading of the Bible will undoubtedly come back again. Now turn to *In His Presence*, p. 35; *God's*

Family, p. 17, and members of the class can in turn be asked to read the section aloud paragraph by paragraph. Questions to be discussed will arise as the section is read.

Tell how both King George V and the late King George VI let their people know that they read the Bible daily. Tell how H.M. The Queen Mother told a vast meeting in London celebrating quarter of a century of the Bible Reading Fellowship, how helpful she found the daily readings. Tell the story of how the Notes, begun to help members of the Communicants' Guild in one South London parish, now go all round the world, and are even published in Braille for blind people.

Issue the B.R.F. Notes 'House on the Rock.' Ask members to look up and read the first Scripture passage, another to read the commentary.

Emphasise the *purpose* of reading. We may know that passage almost by heart already. But we shall read it with care and thought and, using our imagination, picture it all as vividly as possible. WHY? Because that helps our minds to be receptive and God is able to speak to us through our thoughts as we ponder what we have read and try to think out its message and meaning for us to-day.

In this the B.F.R. Notes are a most necessary aid.

Just as *we* talk to God in our prayers, so we must let Him talk to us through the Bible. Friendship *must* be a two-way traffic. So reading the Bible will help enormously to make real and personal the bond and relationship between us and our Heavenly Father.

Say that at subsequent meetings of the class progress in Bible reading will be reviewed.

Rule of Life

Making a rule for ourselves about reading the Bible leads straight on to the subject of a Rule of Life. On p. 95 of *In His Presence* there are the headings needed for a rule to guide us in how we spend our time. It is so easy to crowd God out. Or see *God's Family*, pp. 15 and 16.

We should each, on our knees, decide what ought to be our rule about each of these subjects, to make sure we keep time for them, and then write it in on page 95. For example, under Prayer, what will you decide? I hope you will decide that, God helping you, you will make a rule to pray morning and evening. Will you decide that you ought to read the Bible *daily*? And to worship God in Church at least once every Sunday?

It is for you to decide what is right and to make your rule. It helps such a lot to be quite definite about these things and really make up your mind. Then, with God's help, you will be able to keep it; though, be very sure, the devil will try his best to make you give up your Rule. If he succeeds the great thing is to be sure to start again. The Christian always starts again. He is never defeated for long.

Discuss each heading with the class. With young people it is wise to restrain their enthusiasm and lead them to adopt a very simple rule to begin with. If they aim too high at the start they find they cannot keep it up and become discouraged.

On Giving discuss with the class the solid reasons for planned giving through the F.W.O. or other system. Show F.W.O. envelopes and if possible elicit a decision to join.

Suggest that they gradually make their Rule as the classes progresses.

If time permits, revision and drill.

Fourth Meeting of Class

THE MEANING OF BAPTISM AND THE TEN COMMANDMENTS

Aim: *To relate Baptism to life in the Family of God's Church, and the Ten Commandments to everyday life.*

Baptism

At the beginning of these Confirmation classes you each had to bring me particulars of your Baptism—or Christening, to give it its popular name. This is partly because the Bishop requires me to provide him with this information before confirming. I think you know why? (Questions)—Yes. It is because by Baptism we join God's Family the Church. Where do we find the Font in church? Nearly always close to the door of the Church. We enter by Baptism. By Baptism we are each made a 'Member of Christ, the child of God, and an inheritor of the Kingdom of Heaven.' Let's learn that lovely phrase. (Drill).

There are some very keen and regular churchmen who have not yet been baptised. We have to think of them as great friends of God's Family, doing everything with the Family, but they have not yet been officially adopted into the Family, the Church. They have not yet been 'born again and received into the Family of

Christ's Church.' Look at the Public Baptism of Infants in your Prayer Books. Immediately after the actual act of Baptising come these words: 'Seeing now . . . that this child is regenerate and grafted into the body of Christ's Church . . .' Or refer to Baptism of those of Riper Years if more appropriate.

When a baby is baptised, godparents solemnly promise three things on the child's behalf. You know those promises, because you are going to make them yourself at your Confirmation. What are they?

The Service of Baptism

Let's look at them in the Baptism Service and see exactly what the wording is. (Ask members each to read in turn.)

You have heard of the Baptist Church. Why is it so called? (Baptists do not approve of the baptism of infants, and insist on 'believer's baptism'.) Only when young people or adults come to believe fully in Jesus and want to give their life to Him in a conscious and deliberate act of faith and trust, then they may come forward and ask for believer's baptism. This is usually performed by the believer being totally immersed, right down under the water, symbolising the death of the old way of life, and rising out of the water, 'born again' to a new life in Christ.

The Holy Spirit is given in Baptism—as in Confirmation—so 'Believer's Baptism' seems to meet much the same need as Confirmation. But the Church of England and the Anglican Communion throughout the world retains Confirmation because it was practised by the Apostles, is in the Bible, and has been practised by the Church ever since. It brings God's gift of the Holy Spirit to strengthen us to serve Jesus Christ and make Him of most worth in every department of our life. What were our 'four quickies'? Why should we be confirmed?

It's in the Bible;

It has been in the Church from the beginning;

It makes us FIRMer;

It is the gateway to Holy Communion.

Good. Because it is in the Bible was the first reason. Where? (Acts 8). Let's look that up again in *In His Presence*, p. 28, and *God's Family*, p. 10. I am going to ask . . . to read it. Listen most carefully and see if you can discover in what way *this Confirmation in the New Testament* will be different from *your Confirmation in a few months' time*?

You will only have one bishop. The people whom Philip prepared for Confirmation in Samaria had two bishops (or, more strictly, two Apostles), Peter and John. The bishops to-day, of course, are the successors of the Apostles and stand, we believe, in a direct succession from that day to this. Jesus gave His authority and commission to the Apostles whom He chose. They in turn handed on that authority and commission to their successors, and so on until to-day. We do not believe that a bishop can be a bishop in the full meaning of that word unless he has that direct authority and commission handed down from our Lord to the present day.

We call that the Apostolic Succession, and a bishop must be in that succession to be a true bishop.

Now, once again: the three promises at Baptism which you will make at Confirmation? (Renounce—believe—obey.)

Turn to the last section of the Baptism Service and we shall note the other promises your godparents made. (Ask a member to read.) They promised that you should be taught 'the Creed, the Lord's Prayer, and the Ten Commandments, as set forth in the Catechism.'

What does 'virtuously brought up' involve? Start a discussion on this. Show that it must involve obedience to the Commandments and a close relationship or bond with our Lord. Relate to answer in Catechism.

'See also that *he* be brought to the Bishop to be confirmed by him, so that strengthened with the gift of the Holy Spirit (What is Confirmation?—The Gift of the Holy Spirit)—*he* may come with due preparation to receive the Blessed Sacrament of the Body and Blood of Christ, and go forth into the world to serve God faithfully in the fellowship of His Church.'*

You can say the Lord's Prayer.

You can say the Creed. But can you explain it?

Can you say the Commandments 'as set forth in the Church Catechism'?

Let's tackle that next. Look up the Catechism. It comes several sections after the various services of Baptism and the Thanksgiving for Childbirth which is commonly called the Churching of Women. Notice the

* 1928 Prayer Book.

full title of the Catechism. (An Instruction to be learned of every person before he be brought to be confirmed by the Bishop.) You usually get off to-day with learning the key passages by heart. But you must understand the whole of the Catechism. So you must all read it at home very carefully. Do it to-night in addition to the Bible and the B.R.F. Notes. How are you getting on with them? (Ask a few individuals. Stress again the bed-rock importance of Bible Reading.)

The Ten Commandments

In the Catechism the Ten Commandments come after the Creed. Note first: The Ten (with one exception) are all 'Thou Shalt Not.' Find the exception. ('Honour thy father and thy mother . . .' 5th Commandment.)

The Commandments come down to us from somewhere around 2000 years B.C. Where do we find them in the Bible? The Catechism tells you. Yes. Exodus, Ch. 20. Our temptations are a bit different from those of people of that period—yet surprisingly similar. E.g., 'Thou shalt not make to thyself any graven image . . . thou shalt not bow down and worship them.' You say: Not much danger! I quite agree. I don't see Robert and Jane kowtowing on their knees to a golden calf.

But if we scratch the surface of the old language, what meaning do we find underneath? 'Worship' means 'to make of most worth'. What do some people make of most worth in their lives? Gambling? What about folk (and there are plenty of them) who make time to attend several race meetings each week and fling away a lot of money betting on horses and dogs, but who have no time to make God of most worth either by attending worship in Church or by giving time or money for God's work? Those people have made a false god for themselves and devote a great deal of time to the modern equivalent of 'bowing down and worshipping.'

Now with this sort of modernising technique in mind, let's look at the Catechism and note how it immediately tells us what we *are* to do—not what we are *not to do*. And first in what we *are* to do is put—of course—our Lord's 'Summary of the Law.' Can you say it? . . . (Drill).

Then the Catechism explains what each Commandment bids us do—the positive side of them. You will see that the ten are divided into two parts. First, my duty towards God, and second, my duty towards my neighbour. Let us look at that. Draw out by questioning:

The first four Commandments cover our duty towards God, and the last six Commandments deal with our duty towards our neighbour.

Now I am going to read each Commandment separately and I want you to read the explanation given under Duty to God and Duty to My Neighbour. They follow in almost the same order—but not quite, so be very wary! Then I'll ask you again not in the order they are given in in the Catechism, and see if I can trip you up!

Drill in learning the Ten Commandments and their meaning.

Fifth Meeting of Class

EXPLORING THE PRAYER BOOK—(I)

ITS STORY AND CONTENTS

Aim: (a) *To help candidates to appreciate the Prayer Book;*
(b) *To help them use Collects and Gospels for Holy Days.*

The Bible

The Church has two books which are specially her own. What are they? Yes, Bible and Prayer Book.

The Bible is the Church's book because the Bible grew from the Church—not vice versa. The Church is all those who by Holy Baptism have become . . . what? Yes. Members of Christ, children of God, and inheritors of the Kingdom of Heaven. The New Testament was formed by collecting the letters Paul and a few others, but chiefly Paul, wrote to the congregations he had founded or visited; from the accounts of the life and teaching of Jesus which we call Gospels; an account of the history of the Church for the twenty-five to thirty years between Pentecost and Paul's imprisonment in Rome—'The Acts of the Apostles'; and the book with the hidden meaning, the Revelation of St. John the Divine. And in that order. The Pauline letters were the first parts of the New Testament to be written.

46

The Church selected these writings from the large amount of written material available. Thus the Church fixed the Canon of Scripture. (Explain the phrase.) So the Bible, and the New Testament in particular, is the Church's book. It is the most precious book in the world, and still the world's best-seller. Millions and millions of copies are sold every year and the Bible has been translated in whole or in part into over 1100 languages.

Digress to enquire about members' progress in daily reading of the Bible and how useful they find the Bible Reading Fellowship Notes?

Establishing them in this habit is so important that we must not let this aim slip out of mind.

The Church's other book is, of course, the Prayer Book. It grew out of and is rooted and grounded in the Bible. E.g., when a man is ordained to the sacred ministry of the Church he promises solemnly that he will 'teach nothing (as required of necessity to eternal salvation) but that which may be concluded and proved by the Scriptures.' So there is nothing in the Prayer Book but what can be 'concluded and proved by the Scriptures.' Our Book of Common Prayer in this sense grew out of the Bible, and the Bible has grown out of the Church.

What a wonderful book the Prayer Book is. I don't suppose you have ever explored it? Probably a dull black cover and horrible tiny print—enough to give anyone a headache—have put you off. But both its contents and its history are fascinating. It is a

treasure-chest, when you have the key of knowledge
to open it. To-day we shall have time for little more
than a glance inside.

The Book of Common Prayer

That means the Book of Prayer for everybody—
which is exactly what it is. It takes us from the cradle
to the grave. It is completely democratic. Whether
you are earl or errand-boy you will be baptised with the
identical service and later confirmed*; attend Holy
Communion; be married; be ministered to in sickness;
some day, be buried. The Prayer Book provides for
each of these and many other occasions, and with the
same provision for rich and poor alike.

But we ought to begin with just a word about the
story of the Prayer Book and how we got it. Turn to
p. 38 of *In His Presence*. On that page is a tiny summary
of the story of this extraordinary book. I'll tell you
more about the Prayer Book and that summary will
then remind you of the most important facts about the
Prayer Book when you turn to it later.

The first Book of Common Prayer in the English
tongue was issued in 1549. Who was King then?
(Edward VI. Henry VIII died in 1547.) Previously
the worship of the Church had been conducted in
Latin. Roman Catholic services are mostly in Latin to
this day. This Prayer Book was largely the work of

* H.M. The Queen Mother was confirmed in St. John's,
Forfar, of the Episcopal Church in Scotland, along with boys and
girls from the village.

Archbishop Cranmer. To him we shall always owe a great debt for its stately and rhythmical English. He was a great artist in words. Up till this time the services of the Church were contained in several different Service Books—all in Latin, of course. These services had been drawn up mostly for priests and monks, not for lay people, for whom they were far too complicated. To take three or four large Latin books to Church was a bit much!

So, from these many Latin services Cranmer drew up our Mattins and Evensong; and Holy Communion was translated and slightly altered from the ancient Roman Mass.

This first Prayer Book of 1549 was issued two years after the reign of King Henry VIII had ended. A more Protestant book followed in 1552 through the influence of reformers who flocked back to England from Germany when the boy King Edward VI ascended the throne. Most were probably more zealous than wise and they had to flee again when Mary came to the throne in 1553. 'Bloody Mary,' as she came to be called, was a bigoted Roman Catholic, the daughter of Henry VIII's first wife, the Spanish Catherine of Aragon.

And Mary married Philip II of Spain, the greatest champion in those days of the Roman Church, who later launched the Spanish Armada (1588) against England. Mary brought England back under the authority of the Pope. Archbishop Cranmer was only one of some three hundred who were burned at the stake

D

during her brief unhappy reign. No wonder she became known as 'Bloody Mary'—poor unhappy woman.

Since the first English Prayer Book of 1549, the book has been revised subsequently in 1552, under Edward VI and the Protestant reformers; again in 1559, the year after Elizabeth came to the throne; and in 1661–62 after Charles II was restored to the throne.

Our official Book of Common Prayer is often referred to as '1662'. An attempt at revision, the first since 1662 and the fruit of many years' labour was rejected by Parliament in 1927. In spite of this, parts of this book have been authorised and are frequently used, and it is known as 'the 1928 Revised Prayer Book.'

With great care and scholarship experimental revision of different small sections of the Prayer Book, e.g., Baptism, the Catechism and Confirmation, is being undertaken to-day.

Make no mistake, the English Prayer Book is a pearl of great price. Its services and prayers enshrine the teaching of the Bible, which is also the teaching of the Church. The Church of England is both Catholic and Protestant. Great care and scholarship are required to see that nothing is added to or taken away from the Prayer Book which could possibly detract from its ancient Catholic teaching rooted in the Scriptures. Nor, in the endeavour to achieve clearness of meaning and clarity of language and modern speech, must ancient truth be obscured or modern heresy creep in. This can happen much more readily than most people imagine.

Here then is a book steeped in history, Catholic and Protestant in its theology, easily followed by the people, a book of Common Prayer, prayer for everybody.

For a first exploration of the Prayer Book it's best to start in the middle—which probably seems very odd to you. Actually it is for a simple reason.

The Holy Communion is the heart of the worship of the Church. It is in order to receive the gift of the Holy Spirit and then to be a communicant in the Church that you are preparing to be confirmed. The Holy Communion is the heart of the worship of the Church, so the Holy Communion is at the heart of the Prayer Book, the very centre of it. (Of course, if your Prayer Book contains a Hymnal bound up with it, you have two books in one. It is only the Prayer Book we are thinking of.)

Before the Holy Communion in the Prayer Book come all the day-by-day and week-by-week worship of the Church—Morning Prayer, Evening Prayer, Litany, Athanasian Creed, occasional prayers; and immediately before the Holy Communion, the Collects, Epistles and Gospels to be used at Holy Communion on every Sunday or other Holy Day of the Christian year.

Many people cannot get to Holy Communion on all these Holy Days. They should try especially hard to do so on days like Ash Wednesday (which is the ... ? Yes, first day of Lent), or on Maundy Thursday, the day of the command. What command? (Our Lord's command: 'Do this in remembrance of Me,' given to us at the Last Supper.) Some churches have Holy Communion in the evening that day, as the Last Supper was in the evening.

Special Holy Days

Can you think of other extra-special weekday Holy Days? Christmas Day, more often than not, is on a weekday.

Ascension Day. Forty days after Easter, so *always* on a Thursday. Our Lord's Coronation Day, we sometimes call it.

Good Friday. Explain why many Churches do not have Holy Communion on this one day of the year.

On days like these, good churchmen want to come and worship. On other Holy Days (you hear them announced on Sunday) try hard to establish the practice of using in your own private prayers the Collect for that Holy Day, and then reading the Gospel appointed. It is not difficult and takes but a minute or so. But it helps us to remember we belong to the great company of saints and heroes all through the centuries and of our times.*

After the Holy Communion in the Prayer Book come the 'cradle to the grave' services in the order that most people need them in. Which will come first, then? How do you enter God's Family the Church? Yes, of course, by Baptism.

* *Note :* While pursuing this line of thought some clergy may like to include Ember Days and Rogation Days.

Baptism

There are different Services of Baptism—for Infants, and for Adults. Sometimes a child is baptised in a hurry in hospital, if very ill, so there is 'The Public Receiving of Such as have been privately Baptised.' Never forget the importance of Baptism. Jesus was baptised. He ordered that baptism should be practised. Look up St. Matt. 28, 18-end. Baptism is often called one of the two Sacraments of the Gospel. Which is the other? (Holy Communion.) Baptism is also called a Dominical Sacrament because the command about Baptism comes to us from our Lord Himself, whose name in Latin is Dominus, Lord. Now, next in order? Yes.

Thanksgiving After Childbirth

Commonly known as 'The Churching of Women.' I think this reminds us how many mothers died giving birth to children in the bad old days before the Holy Spirit had led us to our present knowledge of medicine —for which we should give God very grateful thanks, and also for the scientists who have worked to find out God's wonders.

Next comes?

The Catechism

a summary of essential Christian facts put in a convenient Question and Answer form. In former times the Catechising of children and apprentices was ordered to take place after the second Lesson at Evensong. It would make for brighter Evensong if that were still done to-day! Ask class to read the first two rubrics after Catechism. Read the full title of the Catechism: 'An instruction to be learned, etc., etc., before Confirmation.'

Next? Yes! So the next service *you* are getting ready for is

Confirmation

Which is? (the giving of the Holy Spirit to make you FIRM in the difficulties and temptations of life which grow harder the older we get). And next? You need not be in too great a hurry for this!—Yes,

Holy Matrimony (Note its name: *Holy* Matrimony)

Very little to do with the—so-called—'love game' as played in Hollywood by the film stars, who have a succession of marriages and divorces, and which might be much more correctly called legalised adultery than holy matrimony. Our Lord and the Church thought of the lifelong union of one man and one woman producing a kind of home so lovely and so happy that Jesus, from His experience of His home in Nazareth, could teach all the world to call God 'Father.' *That* kind of marriage, Holy Matrimony, needs God's special help. That is why people come to church to be married. But you have plenty of time! Don't rush into it! You want to be very sure, because it is for *always*, 'till death us do part.'

There should be no special connection between Holy Matrimony and the next Service provided by the Prayer Book, which is? Yes!

The Visitation of the Sick

and you may even fall sick before getting married! No clergyman when he comes to visit your sick-bed will use the whole Service of the Visitation of the Sick over you, so don't be afraid to ask him to come. But I hope he will pray with you and lay his hands on your head to give you God's blessing. When we are ill it is wonderful to feel God's love and care upholding and keeping us.

The Communion of the Sick

Actually a sub-division of the Visitation of the Sick but so important we shall give it a heading to itself.

If you are very ill and laid up for more than two or three weeks or so, you naturally want to be 'in holy union with' our Lord (you remember the meaning of the words 'Holy Communion'?) even more than when you are well. So it is very natural and right to want to receive the Blessed Sacrament when you are ill. It does not imply—as some imagine—that you are near death. But there is only one priest to some thousands of lay people probably, so you know he cannot come as frequently as you might like. You can always *think about* your Communion, read the Collect, Epistle, and Gospel and use the Private Devotions in *In His Presence* (pp. 86–88) as if you were there at the altar.

But one day we must all die—there is nothing surer than that. So next comes

The Burial of the Dead

with all the wonderful things it says to us of the life to come. It prays that 'increasing in knowledge and in love of God we may go from strength to strength and attain to the fulness of joy' * in His Kingdom beyond the grave.

There are still some more very precious things in the Prayer Book, and the most precious of all is the Hymn Book of Jesus, or to give it its more usual name? Yes,

The Psalms, or The Psalter

Some of the Psalms, though certainly not all, were written by King David, about one thousand years before Christ. Our Lord knew many of them by heart. He quoted from them many, many times in the Gospels. The twenty-second Psalm was on His lips on the Cross. It's a very wonderful Psalm and very extraordinary, indeed 'uncanny.' Let's look at it and see how it seems to foretell the Crucifixion almost in detail, though it was written hundreds of years earlier. Point out especially verse 1—the fourth Word from the Cross in all probability, particularly when related to the later verses —and the 'crucifixion' verses from 6 onwards until the Psalm changes to a cry of triumph and victory at verse 22.

It was Cranmer who divided the Psalms up into 30 Morning and 30 Evening sections. The little Latin title to each Psalm is a relic from pre-Reformation times when the Church's books were all in Latin and Latin was the language of worship. Not very helpful this for ordinary people!

* Prayer Books of the Episcopal Church in Scotland and the U.S.A.

The last section of the Prayer Book used to be another whole book in itself. It is

The Ordinal

or the forms or services for making deacons, ordaining priests, and consecrating bishops. That is the three-fold form of ministry which comes down to us from Apostolic and sub-Apostolic days: bishops, priests and deacons, the bishops being the successors of the Apostles.

Refer the class to *In His Presence*, p. 26 (at the foot of the page) for more about the three-fold ministry and the Apostolic succession.

Sum up. Drill.

Let the class read in turn *In His Presence*, p. 38, the Prayer Book.

EXPLORING THE PRAYER BOOK—(II)

THE CHRISTIAN YEAR AND LITURGICAL COLOURS

Aim: *To learn the contents of the Prayer Book, its why and wherefore.*

Common Prayer

Last time we started to examine the Prayer Book. Its proper title? (Book of *Common* Prayer, i.e., prayer for everybody.) We rather put the cart before the horse because we explored the second half first.

So to-day we had better study the first half. But first: What is the heart of the worship of the Church? Yes, the Holy Communion. So we find the Holy Communion where in the Prayer Book? Yes—in the centre of the Prayer Book, the very heart of it. But we shall not look at the Holy Communion to-day because that will come later when we come to study the Holy Communion and the day of your first Communion draws near.

To-day we are going to examine the first half of the Prayer Book which contains the provision for the day-to-day and week-to-week worship of the Church (excepting, of course, the Holy Communion which in some churches is celebrated every day of the year, and in the

vast majority at least on every Sunday and Holy Day
and usually on at least one weekday).

So let's get our Prayer Books ready. Again—for the
moment—let's by-pass those formidable-looking pages
of tables and notes at the very beginning (though they
are more fun than you might suspect. E.g., would you
like to work out the date of Easter Day in the year
A.D. 2000? The necessary information is all there in the
Prayer Book tables!).

Having by-passed the tables, we come to Chapter
One, as it were : 'The Order for Morning and Evening
Prayer,' and note that it says under the title: 'daily
throughout the year.' The Scottish Episcopal Prayer
Book says 'to be said and used daily throughout the
year.'

The Daily Office

The clergy call Morning Prayer and Evening Prayer
'The Office' and with the appropriate psalms and the
Lessons from Old and New Testaments they say the
Office daily throughout the year. These services are
not for Sundays only! We do not worship God on one
day a week only!

When people are fond of a person or a thing they
often give it a nickname. Evening Prayer has had a
nickname for a long time? Yes—'Evensong.' 'Mattins'
is not really a nickname in quite the same way.
Mattins was the name of one of the old Daily Services
of the monks—'The Hours'—out of which Cranmer
fashioned our Morning Prayer. Mattins is a very

convenient and good title and we shall use it in preference to 'Morning Prayer'—everybody does.

Two of the tables at the beginning of the 1928 Prayer Book indicate the Psalms appointed for Mattins and Evensong for every Sunday of the year, and for certain special Holy Days too. Which Psalms do you think the clergy use on weekdays when reading their Office? (Cranmer's 30 Morning and 30 Evening sections.) Which Sunday is it next Sunday? Let's use the tables and find the Psalms appointed. The other table—a very lengthy one—gives the readings from the Old and New Testaments for every day of the year for Mattins and Evensong. In England a new table of lessons was agreed upon in 1956, and is now in experimental use. However, let's find the Lessons for next Sunday. (This gives a natural opportunity to discuss their own Bible Reading.)

The World-Wide Anglican Communion

But the Church of England is a world-wide Church to-day. It is much, much bigger, as you know, than just the Church in England itself. Can you name some of the different parts of the Anglican Communion throughout the world? I am thinking about this just now because many of these parts no longer use '1662' or even '1928,' but have produced their own Prayer Books— though these are very very closely based on our Prayer Book. What are some of the other parts of the Anglican Communion? (Episcopal Church in Scotland; the Church of Ireland; The Church in Wales; Protestant

Episcopal Church in the U.S.A.; Episcopal Church in Canada; in New Zealand; in South Africa; other provinces in both East and West Africa; the Church of England in Australia, etc., etc.) This is nothing like an exhaustive list. Each of these is an independent 'Province' of the Anglican Communion under an Archbishop, or Primus (in Scotland) or Presiding Bishop (in U.S.A.). Many of these have produced their own Book of Common Prayer. (Explain how each Province is quite independent and yet looks to Canterbury in loyalty and deep affection.)

Some of these Provinces have restored in their Prayer Books old services which were omitted by Cranmer. An increasingly popular one is Compline—a late evening service which COMPLetes the day.

The Creed of St. Athanasius

But now we must go back to our '1662', or '1928', if we have it. What comes next after Evening Prayer or Evensong? 'Quicunque vult' (whosoever will be saved . . .) or in some editions the title is 'At Morning Prayer' or in yet others, its real name: 'The Creed of Saint Athanasius (commonly so called).' It is ordered to be used especially on Trinity Sunday. I'll tell you more about it when we discuss the Creeds—the Apostles' Creed, the Nicene Creed, and this Creed of Saint Athanasius.

The Litany

Next comes? Yes, the Litany. This is a great act of Intercession in which the people make a response after

each short 'suffrage' or petition. Worship and intercession should never be a 'solo' on the part of the
clergyman. The people should always join in in the
spirit and say aloud the 'Amen'—which means 'So be
it' (Enlarge on this.)

So the Litany is so good because it is a partnership in
intercession between priest and people. In olden days
they loved to sing the Litany in procession and of
course we still do. And it used to be sung in procession
going round the boundaries of the parish—and still is
sometimes.

Incidentally, the Litany was the first part of the
Prayer Book to be put into English. Some years before
the English Prayer Book of 1549 was issued, the crops
failed very badly. This meant starvation for many in
those days. Henry VIII in 1544 ordered Litanies to be
said in all the churches. They were badly attended by
the people, so the daring step of putting the Litany into
English to attract more people was ordered.

The Prayer Book states that the Litany 'is appointed
for use especially on Sundays, Wednesdays, Fridays and
the Rogation Days'. I wonder whether it always is so
used?

Prayers and Thanksgiving

Next comes a section in which '1662' is peculiarly
thin and poor:

Prayers and Thanksgiving upon Several Occasions.

It would be interesting to make a list of the more
glaring omissions from these, according to our way of

thinking to-day? Let's suggest concerns of all Christian people which had not been thought of apparently in 1662? (The list might include missionary work overseas and at home; industry; the unity of the Church; schools, universities and theological colleges; Sunday schools, candidates for confirmation; industrial peace; hospitals, doctors, nurses and the sick; the colonies (no Commonwealth then!); travellers (we should not to-day omit those who fly); absent loved ones and friends; a more Christian home life.)

Some of these are included in the Litany (though by no means all), but not in any of the occasional prayers. If you possess a '1928' we can see how that book has remedied the omissions. What a commentary on the developing social conscience.

Next come the Thanksgivings. The subjects for Thanksgiving are very understandable for 1662 and are quite a commentary on the hazards of those days. Are there any thanksgivings you think should be added? Discuss this.

The General Thanksgiving is a particularly lovely act of worship. If you do not already know it by heart, please learn it. Every churchman should know and use it often.

Collects, Epistles and Gospels

Then comes a long section containing
        The Collects, Epistles and Gospels
used at Holy Communion throughout the year. There is provision for every Sunday and Holy Day, not forgetting every day of Holy Week.

The Epistles are mostly short passages chosen from the New Testament Epistles, chiefly St. Paul's, but occasionally an Old Testament passage is used or one from the Revelation of St. John the Divine. The Gospel passages, of course, are taken only from the four Gospels.

One glance at the Collects, Epistles and Gospels shows that this provision gives us the sequence of the Christian Year.

The Church's Year

You will be just about as lost in Church life if you do not know the Church's Year as you would be in the life of the world if you did not know the days of the week or which month or season followed which. So we must know the Church's Year as thoroughly as we know the ordinary Calendar. And as we study it we shall think too of the liturgical colours which go with it. Each type of Feast or Fast has its appropriate colour; and you will see that colour somewhere in your Church. It may only be in bookmarkers and pulpit fall. It is probably also to be seen in Altar frontal, vestments, and stole. These, too, are set out in *In His Presence*, p. 43, *God's Family*, p. 14.

From this point it is simply a question of memorising. Point out the big jump in terms of our Lord's life from Epiphany to Ash Wednesday and Lent; and again the jump from Lent to Holy Week. Holy Week to Whit Sunday is a natural sequence in our Lord's life. Trinity is a comparatively 'modern' festival probably started by Anselm, about eight hundred years ago. The Church of Rome calls these Sundays the Sundays after Pentecost and has no Trinity Sunday.

The class is unlikely to know the names and dates, let alone the colours, of the Feasts of the Virgin Mary, Michaelmas or All Saints—not forgetting Hallowe'en! Show how some of these holy days are in our secular calendars, Lady Day, Michaelmas, etc.

Make sure that *all know the Christian Year thoroughly*— and the colours. They will enjoy 'drill' in this.

Next, discuss progress in their prayers. Invite any who have difficulties to stay behind and discuss them. Ask about Bible reading. Discuss the passages read in the last few days. This side of their preparation for Confirmation is vital and perhaps it is by your constant interest and encouragement you can help them most. Make opportunities to encourage members. To establish good habits is a very important part of confirmation training.

If time permits, General Revision.

E

Seventh Meeting of Class

HOW THE CREEDS WERE MADE

Aim: *To teach the meaning of the Creeds. To increase a sense of the awe and wonder of God;*
To show how the Creeds grew out of the experience of the Church.

Three Creeds

In the Prayer Book there are two short statements or summaries of Christian belief. We call these the Creeds. There is also a longer and rather different one. Do you remember them? (Apostles', Nicene, and Athanasian.) Where do we find each in the Prayer Book? (Apostles': Mattins, Evensong, Litany, Holy Baptism and Confirmation. Nicene: At Holy Communion only. Athanasian: Placed after Evening Prayer; for use on special days, particularly Trinity Sunday. We will consider only the Apostles' and Nicene.)

Each Creed divides into three main sections, the first dealing with God the Father, the second with God the Son, and the third with God the Holy Ghost (or Holy Spirit) and His special concern, the life of the Church.

Look up the Apostles' and Nicene Creeds in the Prayer Book and note this three-paragraph pattern.

(The Nicene Creed is on p. 75 of *In His Presence* and on p. 36 in *God's Family*.)

The Origin of the Creeds

How old are the Creeds? The Apostles' is misleadingly named, for it does not go back as far as the days of the Apostles. The Creed may have started as a password in days when it was dangerous to be a Christian. It was always a profession of faith at Baptism. Its older form (The Old Roman Creed) may go back as far as A.D. 100.

The Nicene was drawn up at the Council of Nicaea in A.D. 325 (though the later Councils of Constantinople and Chalcedon made contributions to the finished document).*

Note how in this Nicene Creed the second paragraph dealing with God the Son is enlarged to defend the Godhead or divinity of our Lord Jesus Christ, which was at that period being attacked by the heretic Arius and those he led astray. He claimed that Jesus was not God, merely a kind of super-man.

The Athanasian Creed was drawn up at the same period and for this same purpose.

(Appoint two readers at this stage. One is to be ready to read each clause in the Apostles' Creed as required; the other to supply the corresponding clause from the Nicene Creed. With older classes only, a third might contribute from the Athanasian Creed.)

* Only to Senior Classes, perhaps, should these later Councils be mentioned. With younger candidates it is better to give them only the essential facts, and not overburden their memories.

The Importance of the Creed

We are so accustomed to saying the Creed in church that it is terribly easy not to think about what it means as we recite it. Actually it is one of the most exciting documents in the world and contains the most staggering assertions, so much so that some people like to go down on one knee when making one of those assertions or claims. Have you noticed people doing this? Do they go down on one knee in your Church? 'Genuflect' is the word for it.

At which assertion do some people do this?—The assertion that God Himself, who had created this vast and immeasurable and incomprehensible universe, this earth and a million million stars, and distance and space so utterly inconceivably vast that light from a star can take millions of years, travelling at the speed light travels at, 186,000 miles per second, to come from that star to this earth of ours, this Creator God at one certain moment in space and time and history chose to take human flesh by being born into the world of man through motherhood by a Jewish maid. Truly a terrific claim to make! But Christians confidently make it. It is the very bed-rock of the Christian religion. No wonder some people like to bend their knee as they assert such a thing! God is so infinitely greater and more wonderful, more full of awe, than we can possibly imagine Him. It is a great pity to lose our sense of the awe and fear of God. People of old feared Him. So should we, even though Jesus taught us also to think of God as a God of love.

Another important point: People sometimes imagine the Creeds were invented by theologians to puzzle and confuse ordinary people like us. The opposite is the truth. The Creeds are the attempt of the Church to put into the very simplest words *the experience of the Church*, what the facts had compelled them to believe. The Creeds never theorise. They put experience into words. It took much effort to find the right words and phrases to 'freeze' in one short statement and preserve for ever the meaning and logic of those experiences which the early Christians had lived through. So the Creeds are not theory *about* God, but experience of God.

The Creed was a profession of faith made at Baptism by those who had come to believe in our Lord Jesus Christ.

The Creeds were not originally recited at many Services as they are to-day. (Which services?) This use came centuries later.

But, an awkward thing about words is that in process of time their meaning nearly always seems to change. To-day, I daresay, you will feel that several words in the Creeds no longer express what they were meant to, and should be revised. Let's watch that point as we go through the Creeds, perhaps in the Nicene Creed especially.

The Nicene Creed (THE FIRST PARAGRAPH)

The Apostles' Creed reader reads the first paragraph. It's very short, isn't it? The Nicene Creed reader?—What does *that* add? '*One* God.' '*And of all things visible and invisible*' (against Arianism). (Discuss 'invisible'—suggest qualities of character: love, self-sacrifice, unselfishness, etc., etc., the invisible creation —the spiritual world—heaven and hell—the holy angels.)

Let all say together: 'I believe in God—the Father— Almighty—Maker of heaven and earth.'

The Jews had no doubt whatever of the existence of a Creator God who had called the world into being. People of most religions believe *that*. The world cannot have just happened. Chemistry and physics can account for much materially, but very few indeed believe seriously that chemistry can account for moral values. Mankind is different from all other visible creatures in that man has moral values (no animal has them) and man knows he is responsible. (This is a vitally important subject. Treatment of it must vary very much according to the age and capacity of the class. Help them to see that this sense of values and responsibility and appreciation is what is meant when the Bible states that man was created 'in the image of God'. Nothing to do with appearance!)

God the Creator

So people of most religions in the world believe in a Creator God. The scientists say that a billion years ago there was a vast swirling mass of flaming gases rushing through space, that this gradually cooled and quantities broke away to give us sun and stars, and earth. The

Christian accepts what science teaches but asks: 'Who made space, and who put that swirling mass of flaming gases there?' And the Christian knows the answer: God is the Uncaused Cause. He is the Creator of the Universe, and, hundreds of millions of years later, of mankind too. The first words of the Bible are: In the beginning God . . . (Genesis I, 1.)

It is important to remember that Science and Christianity have no quarrel. Great scientists are very often great Christians, though of course some are not. Many are 'agnostics', i.e., people who believe there is a Creator God, an Uncaused Cause, but who also believe we cannot know much, if anything, about Him. There are just a very few 'atheists', that is, people who believe there is no God at all, no Creator, and that the universe came into existence by accident. Atheism raises greater intellectual problems than does Christianity. It's well worth while to remember the saying 'Science teaches us how the world works. Religion teaches why—what the world is for.'

So the first paragraph of the Creed asserts there is a Creator God. But now, something new (at least with the content Jesus gave it)—our Lord taught people to think of this Creator God in terms of fatherhood, the most perfect ideal of loving fatherhood, only infinitely more perfect and more loving and wise than the very best of earthly fathers. Can you think of any passages in the Gospels where Jesus taught the Fatherhood of God? . . . (Discuss.) So the first paragraph of the Creed begins to take shape: 'I believe in God the Father.'

The Father Almighty

The term 'Almighty' often causes misunderstanding. E.g., people say: 'If God is a Father and Almighty why does He let innocent people suffer? For instance, that little baby of a year old when the mother knocked the boiling kettle over him. The baby had done no harm. Why should he have to suffer?' God will not break His own natural laws of Cause and Effect. This is often very puzzling. If God loves us why does He not step in and save us? But if God stepped in to preserve good people from suffering, goodness would cease to be goodness and become mere self-interest instead. E.g., If I knew that by living a good life I could avoid getting cancer or having suffering and unhappiness to endure, then obviously it would be very much to my advantage to lead a good life and what a fool I'd be if I didn't. I should have turned goodness into self-interest, a kind of insurance policy against suffering. No—God lets His rain fall on the just and the unjust. Cause and effect will bring suffering to good and bad alike. What God in His fatherhood does, is to give those who genuinely seek help from Him an inward strength and power— 'grace' is the theological term—so that even in suffering they can still know an inward peace and even joy that can lift them unconquered above the worst blows of life.

(Older classes will want to discuss this. The point that, if goodness rendered us immune from suffering, goodness would thus be reduced to self-interest, helps many to cope a little better with the mystery of 'undeserved' or 'unjust' suffering and a loving God.)

The Nicene Creed (THE SECOND PARAGRAPH)

The Apostles' Creed reader now reads the second paragraph. The Nicene Creed reader does the same. A much bigger difference between the two in this second paragraph!

You remember why the Nicene Creed was written (To refute Arius and those who taught that Jesus was merely a kind of super-man but was not God). What does the Apostles' Creed say about our Lord? (I believe . . . in Jesus Christ his only Son our Lord.)

Short and sharp and to the point! But to refute Arius and his fellow travellers read again what the Nicene Creed says?

(I believe . . . in one Lord Jesus Christ, the only-begotten Son of God, Begotten of his Father before all worlds, God of God, Light of Light, Very God of Very God, Begotten, not made, Being of one substance with the Father, by Whom all things were made . . .) Quite an earful for Arius! (Point out how each phrase refutes the heresy.)

Now we will go on: Apostles' Creed reader. Nicene Creed reader.

Apostles: 'Who was conceived by the Holy Ghost, Born of the Virgin Mary' . . .

Nicene: 'Who for us men and for our salvation came down from heaven, and was incarnate by the Holy Ghost of the Virgin Mary, And was made man' . . .

This second paragraph is concerned to make perfectly clear that this man Jesus was both perfectly a man and at the same time was perfectly divine, part of God's very self, His Son. Believing that, the Virgin Birth is easy to understand. If Jesus had had a human father we would have expected Jesus to be a man only. Because He was also divine we can understand so easily why His birth should have been different.

Continue clause by clause to the end of this second paragraph. Get members to give the passage or event in the Gospels each clause refers to as follows: Crucified for us under Pontius Pilate (equivalent to modern phrase 'in the year . . .'). He suffered and was buried. And the third day He rose again. According to the Scriptures (Old Testament prophecy). Ascended into heaven. Sitteth on the right hand of the Father. And He shall come again . . . To judge both the quick and the dead. Whose kingdom shall have no end.

For summary and discussion:

1. The names of the three Creeds?

2. The original purpose of the Creed?

3. Other uses, early and later?

4. What were the origins of the three Creeds?

5. Their ages?

6. What did Arius teach?

7. What was the answer of the Church? Quote from Nicene Creed?

8. Does the Creed express theories about God or experience of Him?

9. What is the difference between an 'agnostic' and an 'atheist'?

10. God is Almighty and He is a loving Father. Why then should He let good and innocent people suffer?

Eighth Meeting of Class

THE CREEDS AND THEIR MEANING

Aim: *To teach the meaning of the Creeds and show how these grew out of the experience of the Church.*

Why Three Creeds?

First a little revision: The names of the Creeds? Dates? Why was not the Apostles' Creed enough? Why did the Council of Nicaea expand it? How many divisions or paragraphs in each Creed? Which service uses the Nicene Creed only? When is the Apostles' Creed used? We use the Creeds in recitation in worship. Is this how they were first used?

The Apostles' Experience Crystallised

The Apostles and their friends had lived and worked with Jesus for about three years, and been taught by Him. They had been present at His betrayal, trial, condemnation and execution—and incidentally had been convinced that everything was over and done with now that their Leader was dead and buried.

Then they lived through the tremendous experiences of His resurrection and the many times He came to them and taught them during the great Forty Days which followed; they witnessed His unique departure from them in the Ascension; with joy and perfect trust they awaited the Comforter (Strengthener) He promised would come. They found that promise fulfilled to the hilt in what happened at Pentecost when the Holy Spirit actually came to them. Since then the whole of the world, Christian or Hottentot, has been looking at the fulfilling of that promise too. No one can deny the miracle of the transformation of those eleven frightened, mostly uneducated men into leaders who 'turned the world upside down' (Acts 17: 6) and planted the Church so firmly in many lands that to-day Christ's Body the Church, is the mightiest organisation the world has ever seen.

So out of this experience and their interpretation of the meaning of what had happened and what they had taken part in, the second paragraph of the Creed (and part of the third paragraph) were gradually crystallised. These recorded the birth and life and death and resurrection of the man Jesus, but made it perfectly clear that their experience of Him and every fact connected with Him allowed only one possible interpretation, namely that as well as being man He was also God. No other explanation covered *all* the facts.

Last meeting we compared the second paragraph in the Apostles' and Nicene Creeds sentence by sentence, and we related each statement to events or the teaching of Jesus as recorded in the Gospels, or to the circumstances in which the Creed was drawn up. We shall continue that process now.

Explain that in the statement 'He descended into *hell*' the Greek word 'hades' is used, meaning 'the place of the dead'. To-day 'hell' means for us 'the state of the damned'. But this is translated by the Hebrew word 'Gehenna'. When Jesus said to the dying thief on the cross 'This day thou shalt be with Me in *paradise*' it was the word 'hades' He used. So we have 'hades' in the gospel translated 'paradise,' and 'hades' in the Creed translated 'hell'. Dreadfully confusing! No wonder we should like to re-write one or two words in the Creeds.

The Third Paragraph of the Creed

Let us go on then and relate each phrase in the third paragraph to events or teaching in the New Testament. Readers recite the paragraph clause by clause.

'I believe in the Holy Ghost.' To what do you relate this? (Pentecost. Our Lord's promise 'I will not leave you comfortless, I will come to you,' etc.)

'The Holy Catholic Church.' (The founding of His divine society the Church was one of the main purposes of the Incarnation. 'Catholic' means universal: for all people, everywhere, for all time—to be carefully distinguished from *Roman* Catholic Church, which constantly omits the word 'Roman' though it is part of its official and legal name.)

The next phrase enlarges on the meaning of 'the Holy Catholic Church'. It describes the Church as 'The Communion of Saints'. Saints is used in its old sense in the New Testament as 'members of the

Church'. St. Paul often wrote 'The Saints salute you', meaning 'the members of the Church send you their greetings'. So the CommUNION of the Saints means 'the Union together of all the members of the Church'. Now when we die we leave this earthly life, but we certainly do not drop out of God's Family the Church. We still belong to the great company of Christians of all the ages. The great saints and heroes of God are still in the same society that you and I belong to. When we die we shall come into far closer union with our own loved ones who have died before us as well as that wonderful and glorious company of those who have served God faithfully in all the centuries and in all the countries of the globe. We and they together are 'the Communion of the Saints'—the members of God's Family the Church here and hereafter:

> 'One family we dwell in Him,
> One Church, above, beneath.'

'The Forgiveness of Sins.' What did Jesus teach about this? (Our Lord's Parable about the Unmerciful Servant; Peter's question: How oft shall my brother sin against me and I forgive him?; the teaching of the Lord's Prayer.) Link this up with the parts of penitence; being sorry, telling God you are sorry, purpose of amendment. Link up again with penitence and confession before Confirmation or Baptism, if not yet baptised. Link on (by questions) to Self-Examination and preparation for Holy Communion.

'The Resurrection of the Body.' Ask what they think

this phrase means? Admit frankly that at an early period a crude idea was held that God would miraculously piece together and raise up alive once more our body of flesh and blood and bone (in spite of and quite contrary to St. Paul's clear teaching that 'corruption cannot inherit incorruption').

Look up Paul's first letter to the Christians in Corinth, Ch. 15, and consider the passage. Think of our Lord's resurrection body. Help class to see that the phrase means the survival after death of our full personality with whatever form of spiritual body may be necessary for recognition and for the expression of our personality.

'The Life Everlasting.' Explain that 'everlasting' would on the surface appear to mean 'continuing for ever and ever'—but that puts all the accent in the wrong place. 'Everlasting' expresses first and foremost the *quality*, not the duration, of the future life. Its essential *quality* is life with Christ in God. Only in the sense that God is eternal do we believe that this future life with Him may last for ever.

This talk leaves much scope for revision and drill, and the session should end with this as time may permit. Use may be made again of the questions at the end of the last chapter. Frequent and thorough revision is essential—and is usually enjoyed.

Ninth Meeting of Class

HOLY COMMUNION—I

ITS JOYFULNESS AND SOLEMNITY

Aim: *To teach the joy and also solemnity of holy union with our Lord. The names and meanings of the Sacrament.*

Do you remember the 'four quickies'?
(Why be Confirmed? Because:

1. It is in the Bible. Acts, Ch. 8,

2. It has been in the Church from the beginning,

3. It makes us FIRMer,

4. It is the gateway to Holy Communion.)

At this meeting we are going to begin to think about the Holy Communion.

The Importance of this Sacrament

Now, everyone here has attended Holy Communion, so you have a good picture in your mind of the service. But what is the service *doing?*

First: One cannot overstate the importance, the seriousness, the sacredness, and the solemnity of Holy Communion. St. John records Jesus as saying: 'Except ye eat the flesh of the Son of Man and drink His blood ye have no life in you' (ch. 6). We are dead

F

spiritually, have no life in us, except we partake of this Sacrament . . . whenever it may be had, naturally. If you lived on a Robinson Crusoe island where you *could* not receive it, God would not of course punish you for what you could not help. But for us who *can* receive that Sacrament we must not forget those startling and very frightening words of Jesus.

So first: the tremendous importance, the life and death importance, of this Sacrament. Jesus died on Calvary to make us at one with God. (Atonement—at-one-ment). We may enter into that reconciliation, that at-one-ment, which Jesus brought about between man and God, by partaking of this Sacrament, entering thereby into *holy union with* our Lord. Remember what it cost Jesus to make that at-one-ment. It cost Him the Cross. That is a good measure of the importance of the Sacrament.

And second: the joyfulness of this Sacrament. It is the *Holy Communion*. We enter by it into *holy union with* our Blessed Lord. He dwells in us and we in Him. What could be more joyful than that? It is the Banquet of the King's Son to which we are commanded. Here the King's people enter the Royal Presence with joy and gladness. So however solemn the Holy Communion—and it must always be solemn and sacred and reverent to the utmost degree because it is an entering into the death of Jesus on the Cross and a pleading of His death to redeem mankind—however solemn it is, it is also the sacred *joyful* meal which expresses the happy fellowship of God's Family the Church.

When you were Sunday-school children you were probably taught that the Bread and the Wine in the Sacrament of the Holy Communion were food to strengthen our souls, our spiritual lives, just as ordinary food keeps alive and strong our bodies. This of course is true, yet it is only one little part of the truth about the Holy Communion, which is the very heart of the worship of the Church. In each of our next classes we will be learning other facts about what Holy Communion is and what we do when we join in that worship.

But first, some 'quickies' about what we have been thinking about to-night:

1. Its 'life and death' importance. What did Jesus say about it? ('Except ye eat the flesh of the Son of Man and drink His blood ye have no life in you'.)

2. Where is that recorded? (St. John's Gospel, ch. 6.)

3. So, first, the 'solemnness'—second, the joyfulness of the Holy Communion.

   Joyful, first, because Holy Communion means . . .? (holy union with our Lord.) As we say in the service 'that evermore may we dwell in Him and He in us.'

   What is the name of that prayer? (Prayer of Humble Access.) How wonderful that God should come and dwell in and *possess* us, make us His own. What could be more joyful?

Again, we are taught in the New Testament to think of the Holy Communion as a Royal Banquet—the Banquet of the King's Son to which we are *commanded*. What a joyful thrill it would be if we were commanded to attend a royal banquet in Buckingham Palace! But we, God's people, go not to Buckingham Palace but to the Banquet of the King of Kings and Lord of Lords. We enter the Royal Presence with exceeding great joy! And we must never forget that when Jesus gave us this Sacrament, He made it a royal command. He said, 'Do this in remembrance of Me.'

Drill the class until you are satisfied that they have grasped

1. The twin thoughts of the solemnity and the joy of the Holy Communion.

2. Its 'life and death' importance.

3. The simple meaning of the words 'Holy Communion' as 'holy union with' our Lord.

4. The analogy of the Holy Communion and the joy of the Royal Banquet and entering into the presence of the King.

In all this you are laying an essential and vital foundation, often never laid. When you are satisfied they have thoroughly learned this, proceed:

Names by which the Holy Communion is Known

So important is the Holy Communion and so central in the life of the Church from the day of the Last Supper until to-day that it has received many names.

It is useful to know them, for each reminds us of a different meaning or fact about the Holy Communion:

'*The Lord's Supper*' reminds us that Jesus gave us this Sacrament at His last meal with His disciples in the upper room the night before He was crucified. You have learned the Christian Year. What is the name given to that day? (*Maundy* Thursday = the day of the com*mand*.) What command? ('Do this in remembrance of Me.')

'*The Holy Communion*' is perhaps the most frequently used name in the Church of England because it teaches us that by this Sacrament we enter into *holy union* with Jesus, and He dwells in us and we in Him.

'*The Liturgy*' reminds us that in this Sacrament we present before the Father the sacrifice of Jesus on the Cross. His death on Calvary for our redemption is set out like a great sacred *drama*—which is the meaning of Liturgy.

'*The Holy Eucharist*' teaches another vital action. It means 'The Great Thanksgiving' and when that name is used it tells us that the emphasis in the service will be on thanksgiving for our Lord's great act of redemption made on Calvary to save mankind and bring us back into a happy Father-children relationship with God.

The title '*The Lord's Own Service*' in the Lord's own House on the Lord's own day does not appear any-where in the Book of Common Prayer, yet it is full of teaching. The Holy Communion is the one and only service instituted by our Lord and commanded by Him. Surely we neglect it at our grievous peril.

So there is a name for this great sacrament for each finger on our hand. Let's see if we can remember them. Drill.

But there are still other names. The Roman Church (and many Anglicans too) favour a very short, very ancient name—just 'The Mass'. It refers to no special aspect of the service, as the Eucharist, the Great Thanksgiving, does. It is just a short convenient general title. Some Anglicans do not like using it because it is associated in their minds with what are believed to be Roman errors of teaching. The term 'Blessed Sacrament' is often used to describe the Bread and Wine after they have been consecrated on the Altar. The priest may say he is going to take the Blessed Sacrament to a sick person in his home. This is exactly what we read of being done in the days of the earliest Fathers of the Church, as we call the great saints and leaders of the first few centuries after Christ, and we still do it to-day. We do not want illness to prevent us entering into holy union with Jesus. We need that union with Him more than ever then.

Refer users of *God's Family* to the summary of these names on pp. 26, 27—*In His Presence*, pp. 50, 51.

Learn the seven titles of the Sacrament, with their meanings.

General revision, especially The Christian Year.

Tenth Meeting of Class

HOLY COMMUNION—II

KYRIES, COLLECT, EPISTLE, GOSPEL, SACRED VESSELS, VESTMENTS

Aim: *To increase interest in and understanding of The Holy Communion.*

Needed: Prayer Book marker. Communion Vessels and equipment. Vestments.

A Royal Banquet

Last meeting we were thinking of the Holy Communion. We thought of its 'life and death' importance for our spiritual well-being, its tremendous solemnity and sacredness, but at the same time its unique and wonderful joy, because through that blessed sacrament we enter into 'holy union' with our Lord Jesus Christ. We enter His very presence when we come, as we are commanded to do, to the Royal Banquet. Naturally anything so wonderful is the very heart and centre of the worship of the Church and always has been, from the days of the Apostles until now.

A Prayer Book Marker

Will you make a nice marker for your Prayer Book with three or four strands of narrow ribbon of different colours, and bring it next week? Four strands are best. They want to be at least half as long again as the height of the Prayer Book, and should be joined together at the top only. It is very nice to attach them all to a little cross about an inch long, such as you buy in Woolworths or anywhere; or boys could carve them. (Show such a marker.) One strand marks the Holy Communion, one the Collect for the day. There may be a Collect for a Saint's Day to be marked as well, and a fourth strand is useful to mark the Proper Preface fo that day.

Incidentally, as the Holy Communion is the heart and centre of the worship of the Church, where do you find the Holy Communion in the Book of Common Prayer? Yes, right at its heart and centre. Let's look and see. (You can make a little joke to the effect that if a Prayer Book has a Hymn Book bound up along with it into one volume, then that is cheating. Holy Communion will not then be in the middle of the *volume*. It *is* in the very middle of the Prayer Book proper.)

Let's read the full official title:

THE ORDER OF THE ADMINISTRATION OF
THE LORD'S SUPPER
OR
HOLY COMMUNION

Kyries, Collects, Epistle and Gospel

Like most other services it begins with prayers, then readings from the Bible called the Epistle and Gospel. But first the Ten Commandments are said; or first

alternative, the Summary of the Law which Jesus gave;
or, the Kyries, 'Lord, have mercy. Christ, have mercy.
Lord, have mercy.' This is said three times because
addressed to the Three Persons of the Holy Trinity.
Let's examine all these. But note: the Book of Common
Prayer orders that the Ten Commandments are to be
said at least once a month. Are they in your Church?
They are deeply impressive, and exceedingly important.
They give us a standard of conduct.

Then comes the *Collect* or special prayer for the day.
(No one knows for certain the derivation of the word
'Collect'.) Then the Epistle. We sit for the Epistle—
so-called because most of these passages are taken from
the New Testament Epistles or letters, but there are a
few Old Testament passages used too.

The newly-united Church of South India reads
three Scripture passages instead of two—always one
from the Old Testament, then one from the Epistles;
then finally, in the place of honour, the words or acts
of our Lord as recorded in the Gospels. Everyone
stands for the Gospel, to pay honour to our Lord.

Having in the Epistle and Gospel learned more about
our holy Faith, we then sum up our belief, triumph-
antly and thankfully, by saying or singing the Creed.

Which is the Creed used at Holy Communion?
(Nicene.)

Vessels and Vestments

Now, you have worked very hard so far—at least,
I hope you have! So, to do something rather different,

I've brought to show you the Sacred Vessels which are used at Holy Communion. I am also going to show you the Vestments worn at Holy Communion. But first, I want you to look up: *In His Presence*, p. 44 and the picture on p. 46; *God's Family*, p. 20 and later on p. 23. We will identify each article in the picture and that will help you to remember their names.

Priest will show Chalice and Paten, and will demonstrate how they are placed on the Altar. The corporal is spread, the Chalice stands on it, the purificator over the Chalice, the Paten with the priest's wafer on it, the pall over that, the coloured veil over all, and the burse which has held the corporal placed upright on the Altar—as on p. 20, *God's Family;* p. 46, *In His Presence.* Teach the names of each.

Discuss how boys and men can serve at the Altar—a very special privilege—and how girls and women can make and look after the linen corporals and purificators, etc.

A clean purificator for the Chalice and towel for the lavabo bowl is needed for every celebration of the Holy Communion.

Make sure the various names are remembered.

The class will greatly appreciate being shown these articles.

On the Credence Table which stands at the south or right hand side of the Sanctuary (*God's Family*, p. 23) there stand a cruet of wine and one of water, a box (often of solid silver) to hold the breads which are to be consecrated, and last, a little bowl and towel, the lavabo (= I will wash) for the priest to wash his fingers before he proceeds to consecrate, that is, make holy, the Bread and Wine, as the Body and Blood of Christ.

God's Family, p. 23, shows everything in the Sanctuary and on the Altar very clearly. Try and learn all the names.

Now let us look at the special clothes or vestments worn by the priest.* They come down to us from the everyday clothes worn by Roman citizens, because so many of the early Christians were Roman citizens. Paul had Roman citizenship though he was born in Tarsus in Asia Minor, and he was very proud of his citizenship.

In the course of centuries the vestments have become much altered, but it is still possible to trace the derivation of each. The vestments lend dignity to the celebrant. More important, they help us to forget his identity and they help him to sink his personality. He becomes less the vicar you know so well and more God's minister mediating God's holy things.

The priest can put on each garment—amice, alb, girdle, stole, maniple, and chasuble, while a member of the class reads from *In His Presence*, pp. 44–48, the history of each article. (*God's Family*, p. 20.)

Candidates old and young will be thoroughly interested. From examining the vestments at close range many a girl and woman has conceived the ambition to learn to embroider in gold thread, etc., and to do

* Some parishes will put first teaching about surplice and stole here. But it is suggested that even where vestments are not worn a brief explanation of them be given, as in *In His Presence*, p. 46 and *God's Family*, p. 20.

beautiful needlework, to the glory of God. Try to encourage this. Vestments, banners, markers, etc., can so easily be taken for granted until they are handled and explained.

Now it's time for a little drill—some 'quickies':

Whereabouts in the Prayer Book is the Holy Communion? (At its heart or centre.)

What can we use instead of the Ten Commandments? (Our Lord's Summary of the Law.)

Can you say the Summary of the Law?

Or else? (The Kyries.)

What comes immediately before the Holy Communion in the Prayer Book? (The Collects, Epistles and Gospels for each Sunday or Holy Day throughout the year.)

What is a Collect? (Special Prayer for that day.)

What do we do at the Gospels? (Stand to honour our Lord's acts or words.)

What places are you going to mark with the various ribbons? (Holy Communion—Collect for the Day— Collect for Saint's Day—Proper Preface.)

Why is Holy Communion so specially joyful? (It brings us into holy union with Jesus. It is the Royal Banquet in which we enter the presence of the King.)

Why is Holy Communion so extremely solemn and sacred? (Because it takes us with Jesus to the upper room and the Last Supper and the Cross.)

Names and purposes of the different sacred vessels and vestments.

Remind about making the marker.

Eleventh Meeting of Class

HOLY COMMUNION—III

THE OFFERTORY

Aim: *To teach the meaning of the Offertory as the offering of 'ourselves, our souls and bodies', to God.*

Preaching the Word

Last time we got as far as the Creed. Which Creed? (Nicene. Council of Nicaea, A.D. 325). And we looked at the Chalice and Paten and the special clothes of the Eucharist. Have you made the marker?

After the Creed comes the sermon. It's interesting to note that the only service in which the Prayer Book explicitly makes provision for a sermon is at the Holy Communion—the very service where often to-day we do not have a sermon. In making this provision the Prayer Book is emphasising the importance of the Ministry of the Word. Preaching the Word is part of God's plan. There are few sermons indeed which do not contain some word, some message, in them which applies to us, if we ask God's help to perceive that message and truly seek it. To have to preach to others is a very great and heavy responsibility.

At this class we shall consider the Offertory—which is *not* a grand name for the collection! Do not call the collection the Offertory (it is often done!) because although the Offertory includes the Collection, it means such a tremendous lot more than just a collection.

Let's look at the Offertory in our little books and you will see that at a glance. (*In His Presence*, p. 76; *God's Family*, p. 37.)

The Offertory—very simply—means *Offering* our daily life and work to God, symbolised by bread and wine, *offering* our money to God as an acknowledgment that all we have is really His. We are only stewards. And it is good opportunity too to offer our thanksgivings.

The Offertory is all summed up later on in the Prayer of Oblation (which means the Prayer of Offering) when we say 'Here we offer and present unto Thee, O Lord, ourselves, our souls and bodies.'

Let's read that section over very carefully in *In His Presence, God's Family*.

The Symbolism of the Bread and Wine

The order is unimportant. Sometimes the collection comes first. Sometimes the Bread and Wine are offered first (on our behalf) by the server to the celebrant at the Altar. Sometimes we hardly notice that happening because it's done far away from us—which is a terrible pity because it is a crucial part of the action of the Holy Communion. A little Offertory Procession from the back of the church in which two lay people bring up the Bread and Wine from the people and give them

to the priest to be laid on the Altar, helps us to notice
and *use* the Offertory. What should we be doing in our
minds as the bread and wine are placed on the Altar?
The bread and wine symbolise the work which everyone has to do day by day if life is to go on at all. They
symbolise our life and work. We lay our life and work
on the Altar along with that bread and wine, and we
say to God in our hearts, 'I give myself to Thee now.
Please accept this offering of myself, marred and sinful
though my life is and totally unworthy. Please accept
it, not because it is a worthy offering, but because Jesus
died for me.'

Later in the service that bread and wine will be
made holy, consecrated, made the channels through
which Jesus has willed to give us His own wonderful
life and strength and spirit. The priest will lay his
hands on them, using the very words of Jesus at the
Last Supper when He took bread and wine and blessed
them and said, 'This is my Body. This is my Blood.
Do this in remembrance of Me.' Then Jesus gave the
Bread and Wine to the disciples. They were to go on
doing this because it was the way Jesus had chosen
whereby He would come to those who obeyed His
command and be with them and make them in holy
union with Himself.

When we obey Jesus and go and kneel at the altar
rails we are given back the symbols of our daily life
and work, the Bread and Wine, but now they are no
longer symbols only. Jesus is using them as His own
appointed means whereby He comes and strengthens

us and we become more closely united to Him, more effectively His body, His hands, His voice.

The life we offered is given back along with His strength and spirit and we go out from the Church to make Him *of most worth* in our daily life. After all we cannot make Him of most worth anywhere else, except in our daily life.

The Nature of Worship

'To make of most worth' is the meaning of 'to worship'. There is no use making Jesus of most worth, that is worshipping Him, in a nice service in church unless you are also going to try to make Him of most worth in your daily life from Monday to Saturday—at home and at work. So He gives you back your daily life as you kneel at the altar, but He gives to you along with it His strength, and He says 'Make me of most worth in all that you do. I give you my strength to help you.'

Do not worry if that seems confusing and difficult to grasp at first. It is really very simple. If you read page 76 in *In His Presence* a few times it will soon come clear in your mind. Let's sum it up:

The Offertory is not merely the collection. It's a vital part of the action of the Holy Communion because at the Offertory

We offer our daily life and work to God, under the symbols of the bread and wine;

We offer money for the needs of God's Family, acknowledging that all our possessions are allowed to us by God;

We offer our thanksgiving from our preparation.
More about this, our preparation, later.

This instruction should leave ample time for con-
siderable revision, which could range over
　　The names of the Holy Communion.
　　Their meaning.
　　The order of the service up to the Offertory.
　　The Ten Commandments and the permitted alter-
　　　natives, the Summary of the Law, the Kyries.
　　Points about Epistle and Gospel. Responses before
　　　and after Gospel.
　　The Christian Year.

Never assume that, because you have already gone
over something four or five times, the class must now
know it. There are few greater mistakes! Frequent or
systematic revision is essential and classes enjoy it.

G

Twelfth Meeting of Class

HOLY COMMUNION—IV

THE REAL PRESENCE

Aim: *To teach the Real Presence of Christ in His Sacrament.*

Revision

Let's begin to-day with some drill. Sum up some of the things we have been thinking about.

First: The names of the Holy Communion and what they remind us of about the sacrament:

Lord's Supper: Maundy Thursday,

Holy Communion: Holy union with our Lord,

Liturgy: the drama of the Redemption,

Holy Eucharist: the great Thanksgiving,

The Lord's Own Service: in the Lord's own house on the Lord's own day.

The Mass: short, convenient and very ancient name.

Blessed Sacrament: Refers especially to the consecrated elements of Bread and Wine.

What is the definition of 'Sacrament'? (An outward and visible sign of an inward and spiritual grace given unto us.) Look up this section of Catechism. It is quoted in *In His Presence*, p. 51. Ask for other facts about Holy Communion:

Given to us—By whom? (Christ.) When? (Night he

was betrayed.) Where? (The upper room in
Jerusalem.)

What did our Lord command us? ('Do this in remembrance of Me.')

Had the Jews any other experience previously of a
meal which was also a religious service? (Yes. The
Passover.)

The Passover commemorated how God had saved the
Hebrews from bondage or slavery and led them into
becoming the people of God. The Holy Communion
is a means whereby Jesus saves us from the bondage
and slavery of sin and gives us power to become the
people of God. It is the memorial of how this great
act of our redemption was achieved by Jesus on the
Cross.

The Body and Blood of Christ

Now this takes us straight into the Catechism. To-day
most people are not made to learn the whole catechism
right off, as we used to do, but there are certain parts
which any instructed churchman must know thoroughly.

Turn to *In His Presence*, pp. 52, 53 again or to the
Prayer Books.

'Why was Sacrament of the Lord's Supper ordained?' . . . to end of Catechism.*

Drill the class in this section. Get them word-perfect,
if possible. Young people memorise quickly. Now
there is a tremendous assertion in that passage:

Q. What is the inward part or thing signified?

* Quote in full from Catechism.

A. The Body and Blood of Christ which are verily
and indeed taken and received by the faithful in
the Lord's Supper.

I am sure you can all tell me at once why such an
extraordinary statement as that the 'Body and Blood
of Christ . . . are verily and indeed taken and received'
is made?

Yes—it is quoting the words of Jesus from the
Gospels—what Jesus said at the Last Supper when He
gave us this Sacrament. And there is certainly also a
plain echo of our Lord's words in St. John's Gospel
which we learned earlier: 'Except ye eat the flesh of
the Son of man, and drink his blood, ye have no life
in you.' (John 6: 53.) And later: 'He that eateth my
flesh and drinketh my blood, dwelleth in me and I in
him' (John 6: 56.)

Let's turn up that passage in the New Testament and
read the whole of it carefully. Ask members in turn to
read John 6: 47–65.

St. John does not give us the actual words of Jesus
which He used when He instituted the Last Supper,
possibly because they are recorded in the other three
Gospels, and possibly also because he had written the
passage we have just read. St. John, though, records
what the others omit, the account of how our Lord
washed the feet of the disciples, thus giving us a law
of service which knows no limit.

What did Jesus mean when He took bread and said,
'Take, eat, this is my body.' And said of the wine:
'Drink ye all of it, for this is my blood of the new

testament which is shed for many for the remission of sins.'

Theologians of many parts of the Church have written libraries of books about these words.

The Roman Doctrine of Transubstantiation

The Church of Rome teaches from them the doctrine of *Transubstantiation*. They say that any material is composed of its 'substance' and its 'accidents'. Its 'accidents' are those qualities which one can see and measure and analyse. Its 'substance' is what the thing really and truly is. So they assert that when the bread and wine are consecrated by the priest in the name and authority of Jesus, their 'accidents' (what one can see and measure and analyse) remain bread and wine, but their 'substance' is changed into the Body and Blood of Jesus.

Luther—as you will remember from your school lessons—rebelled against this teaching and the abuses of it, and taught his own doctrine of Consubstantiation: that the Body of Jesus is 'in, with and under' the Bread and Wine.

What the Church of England Teaches

What of the Church of England? What does she teach? What do we believe about this great mystery?

The Church of England is so much wiser. She refuses to define in words what cannot be explained in words. She does not attempt to define what change occurs in the bread and wine. She teaches instead the Real

Presence of Christ in His sacrament. The Church of England teaches that Jesus keeps His promise and that He is really and truly present, there, in His sacrament —how, in what manner, no one *can* define. Perhaps the first Queen Elizabeth gave as good an answer as any:

> 'Twas God the Word that spake it,
> He took the Bread and brake it.
> And what the word doth make it
> That I believe, and take it.

Let's learn her words.

Learn the phrase 'The Real Presence'—and its meaning, that our Lord Jesus Christ is present in His own sacrament, even though we know not how. But we believe that though He is *always* near all who love Him and are trying to serve Him and do His will, yet in the Holy Communion He comes in a somehow more intimate and special way, that we may be in holy union with Him, that He may dwell in us and we in Him.

This doctrine of the Real Presence is a most precious thing. People when they are first confirmed come to Holy Communion because they know Jesus has commanded this. He said 'Do this in remembrance of Me.' We come first because it is our duty and we rejoice to obey. But soon, if we are faithful and come regularly and frequently and with careful preparation (we'll be talking about that soon—Preparation for Holy Communion), we shall find that we are coming to the altar not only because it is our duty. We shall find we are

coming because something—or is it Some One?—is
drawing us and we are not content unless we go. We
remember the cry of the blind poet, Matheson, 'O love
that wilt not let me go . . . Read that hymn (*A. and M.*
699) written by a blind man. The world would expect
him to be bitter and angry against the 'injustice' which
allowed him to be blind. Instead he was full of joy and
faith. '*I give Thee back the life I owe . . .*' We can see in
our own lives that 'our hearts are restless till they rest
in Thee'.

We remember again that the Holy Communion is the
Royal Banquet. We know that the King comes and
joins His guests. Oh, the privilege of it—and the joy!
To enter into the presence of our Lord.

So in the Holy Communion we come not to attend
a service but to meet a Person. Let's say that again:
To meet a Person, our Blessed Lord.

Review of the Service of Holy Communion

Let's end this discussion with a quick bird's-eye view
of the whole service of Holy Communion. We can do
it quickly because you should be fairly familiar with its
order by now, through your attendance on Sundays.

Will you follow in *In His Presence*, p. 71, and *God's
Family*, p. 33. Those are the title pages. Note them
carefully. (READ.) Turn on and follow me:

Part One comprises:
The Lord's Prayer,

The prayer that we may worship God truly (Prayer for Purity),

The prayer for the day (Collect),

A reading from the early Church (Epistle),

A reading about our Lord's own deeds or words (Gospel),

A triumphant summing-up of our belief (The Nicene Creed),

The Ministry of the Word (The Sermon).

Part Two:

A very important action, when we offer the bread and wine and along with those our life and work, our money, and our thanks to God (*The Offertory*),

A prayer for the Whole Church (we have not examined it yet),

Now we are invited to the King's Banquet (Ye that do truly—*the Invitation*),

Then, a solemn act of preparation—the putting on a wedding garment (*the Confession*, followed by the *Absolution*),

Words to give us courage and joy (*The Comfortable Words*),

Now we approach the very heart of our worship. We draw near. First we must worship with all the hosts of heaven (*The Sursum Corda*—Lift Up Your Hearts and *The Sanctus*, Holy, holy, holy),

We take off our shoes, as it were, to draw near very, very humbly (*The Prayer of Humble Access*): 'We do not presume to . . .'

Now we are in the Upper Room. It is the Last Supper. Jesus is consecrating the bread and wine (*The Prayer of Consecration*),

We each share the Bread and Wine as the disciples did of old (*The Communion of the People*),

The joyful and solemn act of holy union with our Lord is complete. We sum up all our love and prayers and thanks in the words Jesus taught us (*The Lord's Prayer*),

And now we offer 'ourselves, our souls and bodies' —the only possible response to what He did and gave for us (*The Prayer of Oblation or Offering*),

Or, a different Prayer of Thanksgiving and Self-offering (*The Prayer of Thanksgiving*).

Finally, a great Hymn of Praise mingling the worship of earth and heaven—the hymn the Christmas Angels sang (*The Gloria in Excelsis*),

And Jesus puts His hands on our heads to send us away with peace and joy in our hearts (*The Blessing*).

If time permits repeat this bird's-eye view of the Liturgy from the Offertory to the Blessing. It is important for them to see the outline of its action. Many never see the wood for the trees.

Thirteenth Meeting of Class

THE NATURE OF FORGIVENESS

Aim: *To teach the seriousness of sin and how sin may be forgiven.*

Sin and Suffering

We have been thinking about the Holy Communion as a Royal Banquet—from the parable Jesus told. It always seemed to me very unfair that the king should punish so drastically the guest who had accepted his invitation but came to the wedding feast without putting on a 'wedding garment' (see Matthew 22: 1–14). Obviously this has a wider application than Holy Communion alone, but it also applies to this because in Holy Communion we have accepted our Lord's invitation, indeed His command.

When the king came in to his guests, he saw a man 'without a wedding garment'—and he was very angry indeed. That man was out to *get* all he could, but he was not prepared to *give* even the time and trouble necessary to wash and change. Without bothering about details, that gives us the essence of the story. God has made a wonderful world, He has prepared everything for our good. He asks us to be fellow-workers with Him. But so many will not. They are out for themselves only. They spoil God's plan. Their disobedience creates evil and suffering for millions of people.

The story in Genesis, ch. 3, is designed to supply an answer to the age-old problem: Why is there evil and suffering in a world created by a good and loving God? And the old writers find the fundamental truth that suffering and evil are caused by disobedience to God. So Adam and Eve (which mean Man and Woman) had to leave paradise, and they and mankind have known suffering and trouble ever since in 'this naughty world'.

But God still loves us and still longs to forgive the guilt of our sins and to restore us to our position as sons again with Him. And He can do so because Jesus died for us on the Cross. There is only one condition: we must repent. To repent means literally 'to change our minds'. We have to change our mind about sin, hate it, and long for holiness instead. One or two of you who were not baptised in infancy are going to be baptised and consequently, made members of God's Family the Church. You will naturally want to start your new life in God's Family not with a bad record still against your name, but with a wonderful clean sheet of forgiveness. All of us want to come that way to our Confirmation. We want to put on the wedding garment of forgiveness made available for us by our Lord. Otherwise we shall be like the wedding guest in the parable and that is too terrible to contemplate.

How we are Forgiven

To receive forgiveness involves knowing our sins,
being sorry for them, firmly intending 'amendment',
which means the will to do better, and asking God to
forgive us. Let's look at *In His Presence*, p. 62, and *God's
Family*, p. 29.

I like the picture in *God's Family* on p. 30. It makes
the steps to forgiveness quite clear. Being sorry—telling
God we are sorry—the will to do better—and then God
gives us His forgiveness and the great burden and load
of sin falls off our life.

The first step is obviously to make sure we know our
own sins. Actually many people do not. They are
quick to mark other people's, but put on very rosy-
coloured spectacles when they look at themselves.
Robert Burns said in the Scots tongue, but I render it
into English—

> Oh, would some power the giftie give us
> To see ourselves as others see us.

To see ourselves as God sees us would be more shatter-
ing still. We should have no self-pride left at all!

Self Examination and Penitence

To help us to see ourselves and get a clear picture of
what we are like we ask ourselves—preferably on our
knees—some very pointed questions. We call them
'Questions for Self-Examination'. They start on p. 65
in *In His Presence* and in *God's Family* on p. 29. These
questions fall into two main parts. The good things

we have failed to do: The bad things we ought not to have done. Let's look at the list in *In His Presence*.

They hurt a bit, don't they? But of course they are meant to. We soon realise we are not such fine people after all—indeed that we are a poor lot—or, in one word, sinners.

You will realise that too when you ask these questions in real earnest. You will need a paper and pencil to jot down the sins you must ask God to forgive.

The next big question is: *How* are you going to ask God to forgive? There are two methods. Both—if you are sincere—bring God's forgiveness equally surely. The first way is to tell God your sins privately kneeling by your bedside or wherever you say your prayers; or a very good way is to pay a special visit to the church. Your church is always open every day of the week for just this sort of purpose. It is quiet and peaceful there in God's house. You can take your time and pray very earnestly, and probably the atmosphere or 'feel' of the church may help you to know that God hears you and is with you. The words to say are there in *In His Presence*, p. 69, and *God's Family*, p. 31, and of course you need your list made when you used the Questions for Self-Examination. Making a thorough confession like this will bring you great peace of mind and relief and happiness.

The second way is to go to your parish priest (or to some other priest) and tell him you want to make your Confession. He will not be shocked or astonished. He is quite used to it, because it is in the Prayer Book

(Exhortation at Holy Communion) and a surprising number of people find that this is the way that helps them best to fight their sins. You need your list from Self-Examination exactly the same. Precisely what is done is set out on p. 69 of *In His Presence*. The counsel and advice which a wise priest can give you at confession can help you greatly. Of course it is terribly humiliating to our pride to confess our sins to God with someone else listening. But do you not think that perhaps it is good for us to be humiliated and humbled?

> Remember: The priest before whom you have made your confession to God will *never* disclose one word of it to any living soul. That is the seal of the confessional.

Which way you choose is up to you. But you *MUST* before you are baptised or confirmed confess your sins to God in true penitence. We *dare* not come to Confirmation unforgiven, unclean, without our wedding garment.

Some of the girls are already thinking of the white dress and veil they may wear at their Confirmation. (White is not compulsory but for young people so much nicer.) We must all think much more of our penitence, self-examination and confession. Only so can we come to Confirmation—or to Baptism. What a mockery it would be for our outward dress to be all white and spotless at Confirmation if we ourselves are dirty and unclean within.

After Confirmation we shall have to confess our sins many times in the years to come. There are special

seasons when the Church reminds us of this duty, e.g.,
Shrove Tuesday, the day before Lent begins, so called
because in former days everyone went to Confession to
be 'shriven', or forgiven, at the start of Lent. Then,
next day, on Ash Wednesday everyone came to Communion and the priest traced the sign of the Cross on
their foreheads with the Ashes of the Palm Crosses dis-
tributed last Palm Sunday and now brought back to
church and solemnly burned for this purpose. Hence
'Ash' Wednesday.

Before the great festivals like Christmas and Easter
we shall use Self-Examination with especial care, because we must come into holy union with our Lord on
these great days in the wedding garment of forgiveness.

Note: Arrangements for the Baptism of unbaptised
members of the class should not be deferred later than
this. The points to be settled are:

1. The day, place and time of the Baptism. Many
think that as near to the Confirmation as possible is
best. Explain that until Baptism, persons may be the
most intimate and enthusiastic friends of God's Family,
the Church, but only by Baptism can they become
actual members of it.

2. Who are to be invited to attend. Encourage each
to bring their parents and a few of their closest friends.

3. Sponsors or witnesses. The practice (provided
for in the Scottish and other Prayer Books) of having
the same sponsor as at Baptism also with the candidate

at Confirmation has much to commend it. A rubric of 1662 states: 'It is convenient that everyone shall have a Godfather or a Godmother as a witness of their Confirmation.' But the idea of a sponsor goes considerably beyond this and seeks to find a reliable young person or adult who will encourage and attend with the newly confirmed person for the first all important months and years of their communicant life.

4. A private interview with each of those to be baptised. At this interview the Baptismal Service will be examined in detail and help given to ensure the candidate's self-examination and confession (be it private or in the presence of a priest).

Fourteenth Meeting of Class

PREPARATION FOR HOLY COMMUNION

Aims: *To teach the necessity of preparing to receive Holy Communion; to teach a simple method of preparation and to inculcate the habit of preparation; to decide the frequency of communion.*

The Need for Cleansing

The story Jesus gave us about the man who accepted his king's invitation—which was also a command—to come to the wedding-feast, but did not bother to prepare himself in any way, just went as he was, and did not put on the wedding garment available for the asking—contains a terrible warning (Matt. 22: 1–14.) We too are invited and commanded to a Royal Feast. *How* we go is vital.

We have learnt a lot about the Holy Communion. Now the time is coming close when we shall make our First Communion. The Confirmation—when we receive the ? . . . Yes, gift of the Holy Spirit. The Confirmation is . . . weeks from now. Your First Communion will be . . . .

Before that first receiving of the Blessed Sacrament and before every receiving, we have to prepare. You would not eat a meal at home with dirty hands. You

H

naturally go to wash. Preparation is to Holy Communion just what washing is to an ordinary meal. It's a natural, but absolutely essential preliminary.

The Great Occasion

First a little story. Everyone knows who Napoleon was—the penniless young soldier from Corsica who made himself Emperor of France and dominated Europe for twenty years. At some glittering reception in Paris when Napoleon was at the height of his power a courtier asked him, 'Sire, what was the greatest day in your life?'—expecting Napoleon would reply by naming one of his greatest victories. Napoleon thought for a few moments, then replied: 'The day of my first communion.' It was a wonderful answer. The day when, as a young boy unstained as yet by the world and the lust for power, he first came into 'holy union' with his Saviour Jesus Christ, that was Napoleon's greatest day.

In France and other Roman Catholic countries, for their first Communion, girls dress all in white and wear a white veil—just as most of you will for your Confirmation. Boys wear a special costume, too. I think it's a pity we don't all wear white like that for our first Communion as well as for the Confirmation. They do in some places. It's a symbol of purity—we have 'washed our robes and made them white in the blood of the Lamb'—because our sins have been confessed and are forgiven.

For ordinary Sundays we prepare for Holy Communion by deciding quite precisely three things:

What we are chiefly going to *give thanks* to God for;

What we must chiefly *confess*;

What, or for whom, we will chiefly *pray*, or our *intention*.

Thanksgiving . . . Confession . . . Intention

> ('Intention' is the technical word for what you are going to pray for specially.)

Once again, our little books will help us. Let's look it up in *In His Presence*, p. 57, and in *God's Family*, p. 28.

Our Intention

It does not take us many minutes to think out these three things. What we shall say Thank You to God for; what we must confess, what we shall chiefly pray about, that is, our Intention.

Having these three things quite cut and dried, and ready, and definite is, I am sure, what St. Paul was meaning when he wrote:

> 'Whosoever shall eat this bread and drink this cup of the Lord unworthily shall be guilty of the body and blood of the Lord. But let a man examine himself, and so let him eat of that bread and drink of that cup.' (1 Cor. 11 : 27, 28.)

You will, of course, usually have more than one thanksgiving and I fear more than one sin to confess, and there will probably be several subjects you specially wish to bring to Jesus in prayer. The essential thing is that we have taken the trouble to think out and make ready at least our main thanksgiving, the chief failure for which we must ask forgiveness, and the chief subject of our intercession.

May I suggest that if you have not been able to prepare in this way and have not, as St. Paul said, 'examined yourself', still go to Holy Communion, of course, still go to meet your Lord there at the altar, but for this one time do not go up to the altar to receive the Blessed Sacrament. You are not bound to communicate every time you are present, though it is highly desirable. If you have not been able to make any preparation, do not communicate. Of course it is possible to make *some* sort of preparation if you get to church ten minutes before the service begins. But your conscience will not approve that. We must prepare much more carefully when it is possible. We must have thought carefully about those three things. What were they again? Yes, your *thanksgiving, confession, intention*. What is 'intention'? Nothing could be more simple. But we *MUST* give God that amount of time. A very good plan is not to leave it all till Saturday night. Be thinking ahead during the week in your prayers. You may be out late on Saturday night.

How Often should we Make our Communion?

The policy which he will advocate regarding the frequency with which the newly confirmed should make their communion is a question which each priest must decide for himself. It is not an easy subject. There are so many pros and cons for each approach.

In parishes where there is an early celebration at 8 a.m. and Mattins at 11 a.m. is weekly communion at 8 a.m. to be advocated? Or fortnightly? Or monthly?

This parish may have a Sung Eucharist one Sunday in the month instead of Mattins or on alternate Sundays. Are young people (and some older ones too) to be urged not to take this possibly too easy and lazy way? Each priest must make up his own mind on these questions after taking into account very carefully the circumstances of those for whom he would legislate.

If monthly communion is to be advocated, it is important from the beginning to explain that that means monthly *plus* the great holy days, or else one or two will miss Easter or Whitsunday because it will not fall on the appropriate Sunday of the month! A better approach is to teach the duty of Communion on the great holy days and to have a settled and definite rule of monthly or fortnightly communion as well. If weekly, of course, these difficulties will not arise.

Many priests will feel, rightly, that the really vital thing is to teach the importance of making a rule about this, be it weekly, monthly, or fortnightly—and having after real thought and prayer made the rule, stick to it through thick and thin. Make it clear from the start how many temptations to break their rule will beset each communicant. The devil will see to *that*. And also their rule about careful preparation before receiving.

Refer to Rule of Life—communion is a vital part of it.

Parish Communion

In the growing number of parishes where there is a Parish Communion every Sunday at about 9.30 a.m. the question is simplified, and weekly communion will almost certainly be the practice. The danger here is that frequent communion *may* tend (*must* tend?) to make this great act of worship and self-giving lose some of its mystery and awe. Familiarity will certainly not breed contempt but it does bring real dangers. Perhaps these are best countered by teaching the Real Presence, the joy of meeting a Person, of coming to our Lord; and then by emphasis again and again on the necessity for careful preparation and self-examination, the wedding garment for entering the presence of the King.

The great wisdom of having a sponsor at Confirmation who will encourage and stand by the young communicant in the first difficult and formative years is so apparent, that it is a pity this is not more frequently practised wherever it is possible to find the right person, and wherever there is little support from the home.

Fifteenth and Final Meeting

THE CONFIRMATION SERVICE

Aims: *To rehearse the actual service. Personal final preparation.*

Important Arrangements

At this last meeting before the Confirmation we have a lot to do—and it is all very important:

1. Check up on Baptismal arrangements for unbaptised members of the class who will then be made members of the Family—'incorporated into the family of Christ's Church'.

2. Fill up the Confirmation Schedule which has to be presented to the Bishop with all names, ages and Baptismal particulars (and sometimes addresses).

3. A careful study of the Confirmation Service itself to refresh our memories once again.

4. Seating arrangements.

5. Practise going up to the Bishop, kneeling, rising, making our bow or curtsy to him, and returning to our place. It can look so undignified and such bad manners if this is ill-done.

6. Some Bishops confirm by using the Christian name by which one is ordinarily known. Explain that

where this is done candidates will be given a card bearing that name which they will hand to somebody standing beside the Bishop.

These details are perhaps the least important thing at Confirmation, yet they are still important.

Baptisms and Forms having been dealt with, we practise the movements at the service.

a. If it is not certain whether the Bishop will wish to confirm candidates singly or in pairs, practise both methods.

b. Boys and men are confirmed first, followed by girls and women. Married couples come up together last, and of course, sit together.

c. Boys in front and men behind them are seated on the south side of the Nave; girls and women on the north.

d. Explain where girls and women are to assemble to don their veils and who will be helping with the veils. Latest time of arrival.

e. The girls and women are usually led to their places in a procession by the vicar at ten minutes before service hour. Boys and men come straight to their allotted seats on arrival at the church.

f. Arrange the exact seating plan of candidates, not overcrowding the rows. Make sure each candidate remembers his or her row and exact position.

g. If rows are open and easily accessible both from the nave passage and from the inner side of the row, it is easiest for a row at a time to come out and those next the centre passage to go up to the Bishop first, and then return to their original places via the inner side (not the central nave passage).

h. If rows are open only on the central nave passage, a row at a time comes out but proceeds a few paces westward away from the Bishop, the last candidates out going up to the Bishop first. On return they go back to their original inner position in the row.

i. The little queue of six to eight candidates formed by each row as they leave their seats should stand on the opposite side of the passage to the row they have left, thus leaving free access to their row for those returning from the Bishop.

j. A chair should be set exactly where the Bishop will sit. Two kneelers are placed on the Chancel step. Candidates should practise coming forward singly or in pairs (or both if uncertain), kneeling, rising, bowing or making a slight curtsy, turning and returning to their places according to g. or h. above.

k. Candidates on returning to their places should immediately kneel and remain kneeling while all the others are being confirmed. Many diocesan confirmation service books suggest private prayers for this period. Point these out to the candidates, or instruct them in what to pray about during this time.

Note 1. A priest who is new to all this may consider rehearsing to be unnecessary. He is quite wrong. Practising is essential if the Confirmation is to proceed smoothly and with dignity, and if confusion and uncertainty are to be avoided. Having practised their movements and knowing what they are to do, candidates are free to remember the *meaning* of what is taking place. This is all-important.

Note 2. Often candidates from neighbouring parishes are expected. If, as is possible, they cannot attend this practice, allocate the required number of rows for them *behind* your own candidates. They will thus have seen your candidates in action and are more likely to conform.

The Service

In many dioceses the 1662 form is no longer used. The priest will have obtained a supply of the form of service used.

Ask once again:

What is Confirmation? (The Gift of the Holy Spirit.)

What does the candidate do? (He makes three solemn promises, to renounce, etc., to believe . . . to obey God's holy will and commandments.)

What does God do? (He gives us the Holy Spirit to make us FIRMER to keep these great promises.)

The Service therefore has three essential parts:

The making of the promises. Prayer that the Holy Spirit may be given. Part of this prayer is always the Hymn 'Come, Holy Spirit', which is always sung kneeling as a prayer. The laying on of hands by the Bishop—the outward and visible sign of the inward and spiritual grace given us, God's Holy Spirit.

These essential elements are often preceded by the reading of the account of the first Confirmation recorded in the New Testament (Acts 8). There are suitable hymns. Make sure that the candidates realise these three essential elements. Rehearse the promises.

Last—and perhaps most important of all—discuss with them again what was explained in HOW WE ARE FORGIVEN. Confirmation is a new start. We must come to it ready to start a new clean page in the book of our life. We must come to Confirmation clean. This means seeking God's forgiveness for all the sins of the past.

To obtain forgiveness we must—Be sorry. Tell God we are sorry. Be determined with God's help to do better.

All this involves self-examination, in order that we may be reminded of the many ways in which we have failed, the sins of omission as well as the sins of commission. Make sure that candidates understand this.

Undoubtedly the note on which to present candidates is to impress upon them again and again that the all-important thing is whether they are persevering in their own private prayers and reading of the Bible. Knowledge is useful—but it is the closeness of their relationship to God, built up through private prayer and Bible reading and public worship with regular acts of communion made either weekly, fortnightly or monthly that is going to matter most. All of us fail, all of us sin, but the Christian is the one who knows his Father in Heaven cares, and who, prodigal son though he may be, by repentance and contrition comes back again and again to the house of the loving Father.

NOW
FIND EACH OF THE NEWLY-CONFIRMED
A JOB TO DO IN THE LIFE OF THE
CONGREGATION

INDEX